W9-AAS-058

COACHING FOOTBALL'S 4-3 DEFENSE

Tim Simons
Mike Freeman

COACHES CHOICE

ISBN: 1-57167-159-9
Library of Congress Catalog Card Number: 97-68314

Cover Design: Deborah M. Bellaire
Front Cover Photo: Courtesy of *Dallas Cowboys Weekly*
Director of Production: Michelle Summers

Coaches Choice Books is a division of: Sagamore Publishing, Inc.
                                          P.O. Box 647
                                          Champaign, IL 61824-0647
                                          Web Site: http//www.sagamorepub.com

DEDICATION

This book is dedicated to all of the players and coaches who have contributed to making the Clovis High School football program a symbol of football excellence.

CONTENTS

Chapter

PREFACE

The defensive system described in this book is the Clovis High School version of basic 4-3 defense that is used by many high school, college and professional football teams throughout the country. The book will often refer to the terminology we use to teach our players to execute their assignments and techniques. It is, merely, our system that we use with our players in our football program.

The 4-3 defense employed at Clovis High School is not the only way to play the 4-3 defense. It is the method of playing the defense that has been very effective for us at the high school level.

We spent several years researching the 4-3 defense before we installed it into our program. Previously, we were a traditional 3-4 defensive team. In our research, we learned a great deal from coaches at both the high school and the collegiate level. Lyle Setencich, Phil Snow, Artie Gigantino, Leon Burtnett, Robin Ross, and Larry Kerr were all important contributors to our version of the 4-3 defense.

One of the primary inspirations to learn the defense was Jimmy Johnson's book, *Turning the Thing Around.* Although he never diagrammed his defense in the book, he referred, often, to the philosophy of his defense, in which the defensive linemen have an opportunity to be aggressive. That concept was very appealing to us.

We would be remiss in not also mentioning the defensive coaches at Clovis High School who have put in many hours of coaching, learning, refining, and condensing the reads, fundamentals, and strategies that have made the 4-3 defense successful in our program: Jack Erdman, Defensive Backfield Coach; Larry Kellom, Defensive Line Coach; and Cliff Wetzel, Linebacker Coach.

CHAPTER 1

History and Evolution of the 4-3 Defense

If the contribution of a creation relies on the genius of the creator, the 4-3 defense is probably the one defensive scheme which has revolutionized defensive play. This opinion is universally shared by all with a knowledge and an appreciation of the football genius of the acclaimed father of the 4-3 defense, Tom Landry. Coach Landry's vision and innovations in the thought and philosophy of football led to his modifications of the 1950s dominant defensive scheme into what is now recognized as the present day pro 4-3 defense.

Coach Landry himself traced the genealogy of the 4-3 back to what was then a version of a preseason game between the National Football League champions, the Philadelphia Eagles and the champions of the recently defunct All-American football Conference, the Cleveland Browns. The Cleveland Browns, along with the San Francisco 49ers and the Baltimore Colts were absorbed into the National Football League following the 1949 season.

NFL commissioner Bert Bell arranged the preseason game between the two league champions in the week prior to the start of the 1950 season. In that game, Paul Brown's Cleveland Browns defeated the Philadelphia Eagles, 35-10. In attendance at the game was the longtime head coach of the New York Giants, Steve Owen.

Steve Owen had watched Paul Brown dissect the long successful and popular eagle defensive scheme. The eagle scheme had been the popular scheme for the last three to four years following the end of World War II. Earle "Greasy" Neale devised the eagle defense in response to the offensive strategy of incorporating the running backs into the more and more common passing attacks of the post-war era. (Neale's eagle defense is the forerunner of Buddy Ryan's 46 defense of the 1985 Super Bowl champion Chicago Bears.)

Brown's strategy against the eagle was to flair the backs to widen and occupy the linebackers as he used the ends to exploit the uncovered middle of the field. The result was a resounding victory for the Browns and a shiver sent down the spine of the collective NFL coaches in attendance, including Steve Owens.

Owens' Giants faced the Browns the very next week in the season opener. Owens, known as a defensive innovator around the league, went to work and devised the 6-1 front backed by the umbrella secondary scheme. Tom Landry, the unofficial 25-

year-old player-coach, was left to work out the details of the new scheme. The details were worked out and the Giants defeated the high-powered Browns, 6-0.

In 1954, Landry was made an official player-coach under head coach Jimmy Lee Howell. By 1955, Landry had retired from playing but the father of the 4-3 had visualized the type of middle linebacker he needed for the 4-3 defense. When Sam Huff arrived in training camp, Landry realized he had found his prototype middle linebacker, and he then transformed the 6-1 umbrella into the pro 4-3.

The defensive theory of the time was one of containment first and pursuit second. Containing the edge would drive the ballcarrier to the middle of the field and into the pursuit. Landry reversed this philosophy and placed the emphasis on inside-out pursuit driving the ball to the containment. The job of the Landry 4-3 four defensive linemen was to use up or occupy the five offensive linemen, thus allowing the middle linebacker the freedom to roam the field and wreck havoc. Additionally, the presence of the two outside linebackers (the advantage of the eagle) was welded with the umbrella coverage scheme to provide blanket pass coverage. The 4-3 defense was born.

In Bob St. John's book, *The Landry Legend: Grace Under Pressure*, Landry described his thoughts in designing the front: "The 4-3 was a combination of the eagle defense and the umbrella. The eagle defense had begun taking on a 4-3 look because they'd put an extra back in for a linebacker to help on passing downs. He'd be standing up. It was becoming obvious to me that the thing to do was keep the ends dropped off, covering the flare areas, making them linebackers."

The current trend of the college 4-3 is to move the front to a slide look. The 4-3 base front we use at Clovis High School is typical of the college 4-3 alignment.

Ironically, Landry made a telling prediction in 1959 about the future of the 4-3. Landry predicted the 4-3 would in some way evolve into a gap control front such as the slide. Landry went on to say the offenses of the future would then be faced with the difficult task of developing strategies to combat the slide 4-3 front.

Over three decades later, Landry is proven to be a prophet of the game as well as a founding father. Offensive coordinators across the country are scratching their heads while playing catch-up in their quest to outflank the 4-3 alignment.

CHAPTER 2

Understanding the 4-3 Defense

The 4-3 defense used at Clovis High School is a model of the 4-3 defense that is presently the most popular 7-man front scheme in all levels of play.

During the Miami Hurricane domination of the Division I ranks, the front was known as the Miami front. Many coaches today identify the front alignment with the "Miami Front" moniker.

Our 4-3 defense uses the college 4-3 alignment. The early 4-3 defenses of the Landry era used a solid alignment on the tight-end side with the strongside outside linebacker aligned on the tight end and the defensive end squeezed down over the tackle. That front was known as the pro 4-3. In the '60s, teams moved the end out on the tight end and moved the outside linebackerback off the line of scrimmage into what most people recognize as a 4-3 alignment. Because the high-profile college teams of the era ran this newer 4-3 look, that alignment became known as the college 4-3. The pro 4-3 and the '60s era college 4-3 were similar in many regards. The most distinctive quality shared by the fronts was the two gap control technique of the front, especially the tackles.

The success of the Miami Hurricanes' slide look began a wave of defensive coaches moving the front to a gap control slide front. The slide front, also known as the college 4-3, allows the defensive linemen to play more aggressively. Because the linemen know which gap is their responsibility prior to the snap, the linemen can attack the man in front of them with a leverage arm free in their responsible gap. The two gap control philosophy calls for the defensive linemen to read the movement of the two offensive linemen in front of them and then react to their action. The two gap control defensive lineman's goal was to keep the offensive lineman off the linebackers. Defensive linemen in the 4-3 are free to attack on the snap. Attacking on the snap forces the offensive linemen to react to the defensive linemen instead of vice versa. The front four of the 4-3 create a new line of scrimmage with their attacking style. An attacking style of play from the front four allows the less talented defensive linemen to dominate the line of scrimmage. The reading style is suitable for large sized and talented defensive linemen. Even when the personnel fits, the reading style can be blocked. The two gap front four technique is becoming a relic as the slide front allows the less talented defensive linemen to dominate the line of scrimmage.

The 4-3 front and its slide philosophy combine with a quarters coverage scheme to make the defense a tough scheme to move the chains against. Cover 4, the base coverage of our 4-3 defensive scheme, uses a man-to-man coverage out of the corners on the edge with two safeties playing a quarters alignment and zone coverage in support. The linebackers provide man underneath help as the safeties cover 1/4 to 1/2 of the field in a matchup principle based upon the release of the number 2 receiver. The safeties also provide run support and force to their side. The coverage scheme also has built-in checks against certain formations. No formation can force the 4-3 to lose a numbers advantage in the box, nor lose a coverage advantage on the edge. The unique style of playing the base coverage confuses quarterback reads as routes which should be open are choked off. The base characteristics of our 4-3 defense are tight man-to-man coverage with zone help and seven in the box.

OVERVIEW OF THE "COUGAR 4-3" DEFENSE

In general terms, the defense features a seven-man front with four down linemen and three linebackers. The linemen use three point stances and are intensely drilled in upfield charging. The linebackers line up in a two-point stance 4 to 4.5 yards off the line of scrimmage. The basic secondary coverage in the 4-3 defense is Cover 4. It is based on creating a nine-man front to combat all run plays and defending pass plays in a manner similar to a "five under, two-deep" man coverage. If an opponent uses a twins or trips formation, the defense will change from Cover 4 to another coverage: a halves coverage, a thirds coverage, or a man-free coverage. The same alternative coverage can be used for both twins and trips formations. Therefore, when Cover 4 is called in the huddle, the twins/trips coverage is included (i.e., Cover 42).

The standard defensive alignment in the 4-3 is called basic Cover 4. Blitz and line stunts are essential. A number of blitzes and line stunts that can be called will be described later in the book.

PHILOSOPHY OF THE 4-3 DEFENSE

The philosophy of the 4-3 defense employed by Clovis High School incorporates three basic concepts: quickness, simplicity, and aggression. First of all, the defense should have players on the field who can run with quickness and speed in order to combat today's more sophisticated offenses. A defense that relies on quickness and speed requires less size and muscle than many traditional defenses that emphasize neutralizing blockers, compressing down blocking schemes, and protecting inside linebackers with defensive linemen. The intent of this defense is to force running plays to the sidelines where defensive quickness can minimize productivity, and to defend passing plays with severe pressure from defensive rushers attacking the passer while outnumbering the pass receivers in the pattern with pass defenders.

The second concept in the philosophy of the 4-3 defense is simplicity in alignments. The defense is not a multiple defense. The defensive players line up the same way on almost every snap. As a result, the players are not hampered by the need to think about their positioning. Once the players learn their base alignments, assignments, and reactions they can become very aggressive in their play. The primary variations in the defense come in the form of blitzes and line stunts.

The third concept of the philosophy of this defense is aggression. The role of the defensive linemen epitomizes this concept. Unlike traditional two gap defensive linemen, the 4-3 defensive linemen are in an upfield charge on every down. Pass rush pressure on the quarterback will exist on every down. The defensive linemen are not responsible for protecting the linebackers from offensive linemen. Instead, the defensive linemen line up on the edge of the offensive linemen, get off on the snap of the ball, get upfield, and make plays. They never squeeze down on kick-out blocks, a technique that requires outstanding strength and power, but come under all kick-out blocks. This technique allows them to spill running plays to the outside. Finally, they always line up on the same side. For example, the left defensive end lines up on the left side every down. This consistency facilitates the development of their various reads and reaction techniques and gives them a sense of security because they never have to line up in an unfamiliar area. This sense of security helps create a confident, well-prepared, and highly aggressive defensive front.

ADVANTAGES OF THE 4-3 DEFENSE

In many defenses outside linebackers line up on the line of scrimmage in a two-point stance where they defend both pass and run plays. On pass plays, they may be asked to drop to a zone or rush the quarterback. In the college 4-3 defense, the linebackers always line up off the ball facilitating their pass drops. The pass rushers are the four down linemen who always line up in a three-point stance in order to facilitate their get-off.

Zone blocking this version of the 4-3 defense is difficult because the defensive linemen are on the edge of the offensive linemen and are getting upfield. On the onside of a zone play, the defensive linemen are very difficult to reach block. On the backside of the zone play, they are very difficult to cut-off.

The preferred physical characteristic for the outside linebackers is speed, not power. As a result, formation adjustments and coverage variations are relatively easy compared to some traditional defensive structures.

The 4-3 defense highlights the single high-profile linebacker. Other defensive schemes rely on the combined talents of two inside linebackers. The offense can usually handle one great linebacker when he plays to one side of the ball. The 4-3 alignment allows the coach to place the one outstanding linebacker in the middle at a position where he can contribute to stopping the run on both sides of the ball. In addition, the 4-3 supports this one great linebacker by aligning another linebacker to each side in support of the middle linebacker.

PERSONNEL REQUIREMENTS FOR THE 4-3 DEFENSE

Because of its emphasis on quickness, the requirements for personnel in the 4-3 defense are somewhat different from those of a more traditional defense. Quickness, athleticism, and strength are important for the four down linemen. They must learn to quickly react to the blocking schemes while on the move. They are not in the game to protect the linebackers. They are in the game to make plays themselves. Ex-linebackers often make good defensive linemen in this scheme.

Coaches using the 4-3 defense should look for a traditional middle linebacker. He should have size, power, and quickness in order to stop the inside running game and give the defensive front the strength to take on the offensive linemen face to face. The middle linebacker is often a defensive captain. In order to fulfill his duties, he should be capable of recognizing offensive formations and patterns and advising his teammates to make the appropriate adjustments.

Outside linebackers are "hybrids" who resemble defensive backs more than traditional linebackers. Size and power are beneficial, but not the primary characteristic a coach should look for. Instead, coaches should select candidates with speed and toughness, since the job of the outside linebackers is to prevent running backs from turning the corner after being forced outside. The outside linebackers should be good pass defenders, as well as disciplined players willing to hold their position and wait for plays to develop when necessary.

Speed is a critical characteristic of players in the secondary. Both the safeties should be good pass defenders who can also defend the run just like linebackers. The cornerbacks should be the team's best pass defenders as well as two of the quickest players. Cornerbacks are not often called upon to defend against the run, but should be strong enough to contest the wide receiver for the pass. All the defensive backs should have the ability to recognize offensive formations and patterns and adjust accordingly. They should be capable of intercepting a pass as well as making an open field tackle.

It is also important for a coach to decide whether to assign right-side and left-side positions or strongside and weakside positions. As stated earlier, the 4-3 defense involves right-side and left-side positions. Players learn the techniques needed to play both the strongside and the weakside, and then line up to either the left or right of the center. Traditionally, positions have been assigned based on the strongside and weakside. For the defensive front, the strongside is the side on which the tight end is aligned. For the secondary, the strongside is the side with the most receivers. Against a balanced formation, the secondary determines the strongside by the ball position. If the ball is in the middle of the field, the strongside is to the defensive left. If the ball is on the hash mark, the strongside is the wide side of the field. If the formation has no tight end, the defensive front determines the strongside of the field using the same guidelines as the secondary. The primary drawback of alignments based on the strongside and weakside is that if the offense shifts players and changes the strength of the formation, the defensive players must switch sides as well, since each player is trained only in one type of technique. This switch can leave the defense vulnerable.

CHAPTER 3

Basic 4-3, Cover 4

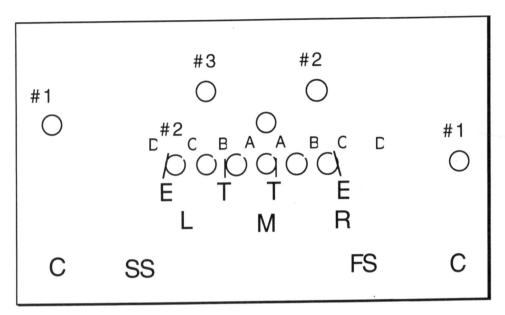

Diagram 3-1.
Position designations and alignments.

The following positions descriptions refer to Diagram 3-1, shown above.

E—End. The left end is always left. The right end is always right. If there is a tight end to his side, the defensive end lines up in a 9 technique. If there is a split end he lines in a 5 technique on the tackle. If there are two tight ends, the end away from strength stays in a 5 technique on the tackle.

T—Tackle. The left tackle lines up on the left and the right tackle on the right. They line up in either a 1 technique or a 3 technique.

L & R—Lazor & Razor. The outside linebackers always line up on the same side—Lazor on the left and Razor on the right-in wide C gap alignment. They are 4.5 yards off the line of scrimmage.

M—Mike. The middle linebacker lines up directly over the center. At times, there will be some slight variations in his alignment. He lines up four yards off the line of scrimmage.

C—Cornerback. The cornerbacks are outside deep defenders who often play man-to-man on the wide receivers. The depth of their alignment varies.

SS—Strong Safety. The strong safety lines up eight to twelve yards deep on the strong side of the formation. He is often counted on for support versus run plays and is a halves player versus pass plays.

FS—Free Safety. The free safety lines up eight to twelve yards deep on the side away from the strong safety. If the play comes to his side, his responsibilities versus both the run and the pass are the same as those of the strong safety.

Gap Designations

A GAP	Between the center and the guard.
B GAP	Between the guard and the tackle.
C GAP	Between the tackle and the tight end; outside the tackle versus no tight end.
D GAP	Outside the tight end; the wide outside area versus no tight end.

Receiver Designation

#1 Receiver	Widest receiver on each side of the formation.
#2 Receiver	The next receiver inside of #1 receiver.
#3 Receiver	The next receiver inside of #2 receiver.
#4 Receiver	A #4 receiver can exist in a trips formation when the remaining back releases to the trips side.

Technique Definition

0 Technique	Head-up alignment on the center.
1 Strong/Weak*	Strongside or weakside shade alignment on center.
1 Technique*	Inside shade alignment on guard.
2 Technique	Head-up alignment on guard.
3 Technique	Outside shade alignment on guard.
4 Technique	Inside shade alignment on tackle.
6 Technique	Head-up alignment on tackle.
5 Technique	Outside shade alignment on tackle.
7 Technique	Inside shade alignment on tight end.
8 Technique	Head-up alignment on tight end.
9 Technique	Outside shade alignment on tight end.
*1 Technique	May be aligned on either the center or guard.

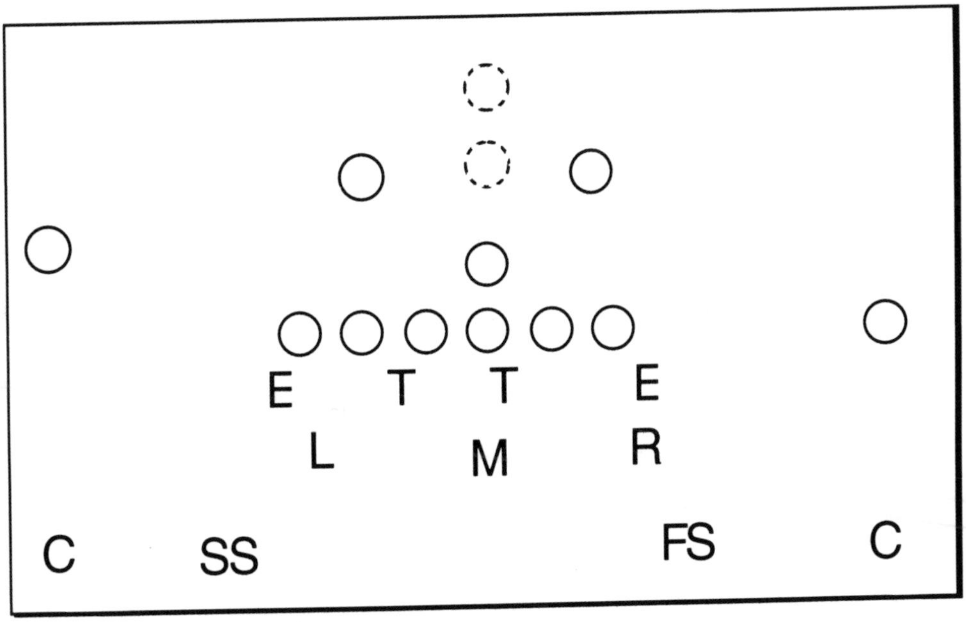

Diagram 3-2.
Right/left positions are relative to Diagram 3-2.

POSITION	ALIGNMENT	TECHNIQUE	KEY	RUN TO	RUN AWAY	PASS
Right End	5 Technique	Base	Tackle	B or C Gap	Trail	Contain
Right Tackle	1 Technique	Base	Center	A Gap	Pursue	Inside Rush
Left Tackle	3 Technique	Base	Guard	A or B Gap	Pursue	Inside Rush
Left End	9 Technique	Base	Tight End	C or D Gap	Trail	Contain
Razor LB	5 Technique	Base	LT, LG	B or C Gap	Pursue	#2 Receiver
Mike LB	0 Technique	Base	FB/Flow	A, B, or C Gap	NA	#3 Receiver
Lazor LB	7 Technique	Base	TE, RT	C or D Gap	Pursue	#2 Receiver
Cornerbacks Cover #1	Inside Receiver	#1	Man/Man vs. Crack	Receiver Reverse	NA unless M/M	Cutback &
Strong Safety	Outside #2 Receiver	Read & React	#2	Outside Support	Cutback & Reverse	1/2 Field
Free Safety	Outside Left Tackle	Read & React	Backfield	Outside Support	Cutback & Reverse	1/2 Field

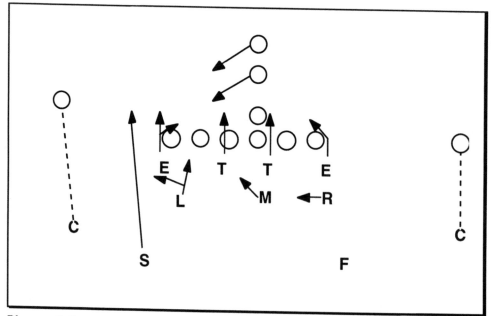

Diagram 3-3.
Run strong.

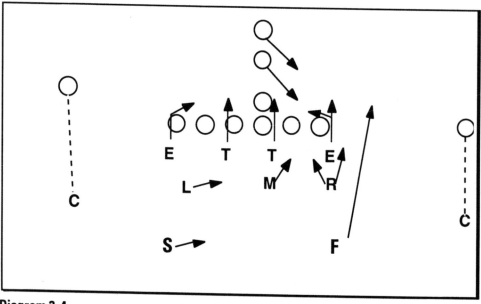

Diagram 3-4.
Run weak.

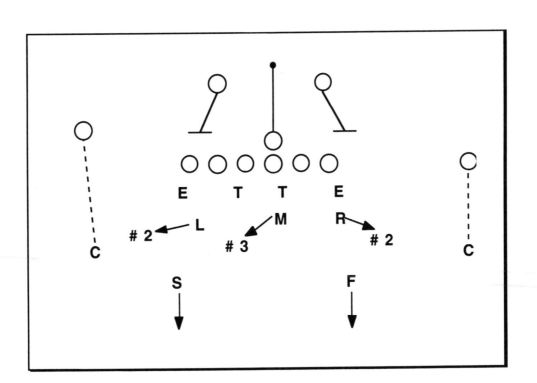

Diagram 3-5.
Pass.

TWO TIGHT END ADJUSTMENTS

Versus one back set. The end away from strength lines up in a 5 technique on the tackle. The outside linebacker on that side lines up on the line of scrimmage in a pro 4-3 alignment (Diagram 3-6).

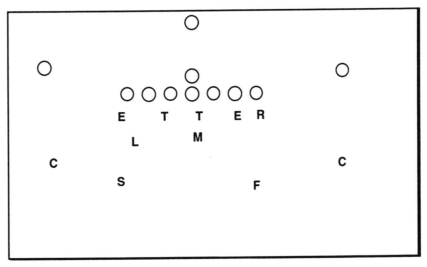

Diagram 3-6.
Versus two tight ends—ace-back sets.

Versus two back set. The end away from strength lines up in a 5 technique. The cornerback on that side closes down and lines up on the line of scrimmage just outside of the tight end. The cornerback, the near outside linebacker, and the free safety check into a Cover 2 (Diagram 3-7).

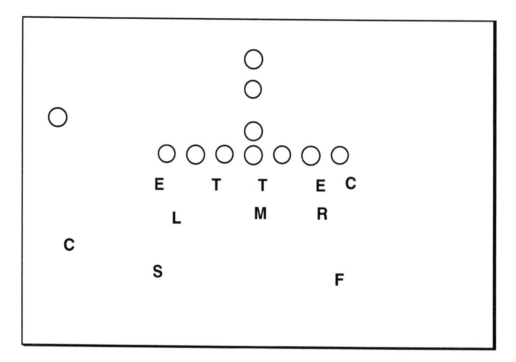

Diagram 3-7.
Versus two tight ends—two-back set.

CHAPTER 4

Defensive Linemen

FUNDAMENTALS

Stance

The key to the 4-3 defense is penetration, so all defensive linemen are in a rush stance with inside foot back and inside hand on the line of scrimmage. Defensive linemen are to crowd the line of scrimmage as much as the referee will allow. Their feet should be perpendicular to the line of scrimmage with the outside knee up under their rib cage. Their weight should be shifted forward to the up foot and down hand. In a good ready position, the defensive lineman is up on the balls of his feet and stabilized on the fingers tips of the down hand. Defensive linemen should have their butt down so their back is flat and parallel to the ground and he is ready to explode across the line of scrimmage as soon as the ball moves. The ball is the trigger. When it pulls, the linemen get off.

Get Off

At the snap of the ball, the linemen immediately replace their down hand with their back foot and run to where the ball is going to be. They determine where the ball is going to be by being familiar with and reading the blocking scheme. Recognizing blocking schemes and running to the ball is an important technique that must be mastered by defensive linemen to make this defense work successfully. Defensive linemen must penetrate the line of scrimmage run to the ball.

Getting off on the snap of the ball is a skill the coach must emphasize on a daily basis. Most successful 4-3 defensive line coaches start the practice with a drill designed to sharpen the take-off ability of the defensive lineman. The 4-3, like other successful attack 4-3 schemes, depends on the cat-like reaction of the defensive tackles and ends to the movement of the ball.

Cat-like reaction to the ball movement requires constant reinforcement from the defensive line coach. The line coach should start all drills with the movement of a football, rather that with a voice or whistle command. In the early stages of training, the coach should rely solely on ball movement in silence. Once the athlete sharpens his reaction skills, the defensive coach may use simulated cadences in addition to the ball movement. However, in no circumstances should the coach neglect ball movement key in any of his defensive line drills.

Coaching techniques for reinforcing the ball movement reaction for the defensive lineman include using a nerf ball for all drills and using a string or lead to jerk the ball from a remote position. The use of the string or lead allows the coach to stand near the drill and more easily evaluate the lineman's drill technique.

ALIGNMENTS AND RESPONSIBILITIES

For the defensive front, strength is called (Right or Left) based on the position of the tight end. If there are two tight ends, the strength is called per game plan strategy. Certain alignments and techniques will change versus two tight ends. All defensive linemen line up on the shade of a man so they can read as they penetrate.

Basic Shades Versus Tight End Left Formation
The basic shades of the 4-3 defense are the 3 technique tackle, the 1 technique weak tackle, the 9 technique end, and the 5 technique end. The 9 technique end and the 3 technique tackle are located toward the front strength declaration. The 1 technique weak tackle and the 5 technique end are located opposite the front strength declaration.

If the strength is declared to the defensive right, then the right end plays a 9 technique and the right tackle plays a 3 technique. The left tackle reacts to the linebacker's declaration of Right by aligning a 1 technique weak. The left end aligns in a 5 technique.

If the strength is declared to the defensive left, then the left end plays a 9 technique and the left tackle plays a 3 technique. The right tackle reacts to the linebacker's declaration of Left by aligning in a 1 technique weak. The right end aligns in a 5 technique.

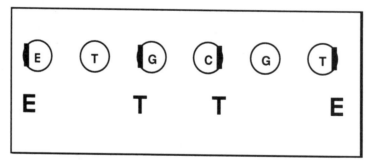

Diagram 4-1.

The strongside defensive end is a 9 technique player. He must key the block of the tight end as he moves upfield on the snap of the ball. His first responsibility is to not get hooked. Getting off quickly on the snap of the ball will go a long way in defeating the hook block. Also, the defensive end may slightly widen his alignment on the tight end if he is having trouble with the hook block. Ideally, the defensive end should drive the hook blocker backward and turn his shoulders perpendicular to the line of scrimmage. On the snap of the ball, the 9-technique end will step with his inside foot to the outside foot of the tight end. During that first step, he must recognize the hook block attempt. He should then pivot slightly on his inside foot to allow his second step (performed with his outside foot) to have some width to it. He cannot allow the tight end to acquire outside leverage. During his second step, he should punch the outside shoulder of the blocker with his outside hand, forcing the blocker's shoulders backwards.

He must then rip through and past the hook blocker with his inside arm. His feet must continue moving upfield and outside, as the battle with the hook blocker continues. All of the defensive linemen in the defense must drill daily on reacting and defeating the hook blocker.

Many blocking schemes exist where the tight end blocks inside toward the ball. By the time the 9-technique takes his second step, he should have recognized the down block. He must immediately pivot on the outside foot and make a turn inside. He knows that a very good chance exists that somebody is coming to kick him out. It could be a near halfback. It could be a fullback. It could also be either the onside or offside guard. No matter who it is, the 9 technique should use what is called the "wrong shoulder" technique. This technique is executed by driving the outside arm to the inside thigh of the blocker. It is not a passive action. The end must aggressively attack the blocker, coming underneath his block, but making contact.

The second phase of the technique requires the defender to square his body up while driving his outside arm and fist in an upward punching motion. He then runs upfield through the inside of the blocker. This follow-through creates the "bubbling" effect that is designated to close the C gap and deny the ball carrier an off-tackle running lane.

The 9-technique player must be drilled on attacking all forms of kick out blockers. Whether the blocker is a guard or a back, the technique is the same. However, since the blocker can come from different positions the angle and the timing of the collision varies with the blocker, the defensive line coach must recreate these situations in his drills.

The third block by the tight end that the 9 technique must be able to react to is the wall block. The wall block means that the ball is being run somewhere to the inside of the tight end. First of all, the tight end must squeeze the wall block by pushing hard off his second step. Second, a decision must now be made whether the defender should come across the face of the wall blocker or go behind the block? For gap control purposes, we prefer all defensive linemen to squeeze and then go behind the wall block in an attempt to get to the ball carrier. However, if the wall blocker has beaten the defensive lineman to the punch and has good position, the defensive linemen needs at least several steps upfield to get around the block. In that case, it is time to come across the face of the wall blocker. Also, an integral part of the process of properly reacting to the wall block is to look in the backfield to determine where the ball is going. This information will also help the defensive linemen determine whether he should go around, come across, or just continue to squeeze the wall block. Once the 9 technique has mastered the reactions to being blocked by the tight end, he is ready to play the running game.

The 9 technique has another set of responses and assignments versus pass plays. He provides pressure with containment against the pass. As stated earlier, if the tight end releases inside, whether it be to block or run a pass pattern, the 9 technique pivots and looks inside. If the offensive tackle pops out and back, the 9 technique knows it is a pass play. The first thing the 9 technique does in his pass rush mode is to drive to a point three yards deep while focusing on the quarterback, but seeing the offensive tackle. At the 3-yard point, the 9 technique must make a decision regarding which technique he will use to clear the blockers.

The drive of the 9 technique away from the offensive tackle and upfield will usually force the tackle to open his shoulders. The offensive tackle will attempt to close the distance by hinging toward the 9 technique. Once the offensive tackle opens his shoulders and hinges, the 9 technique has gained the advantage. Upon recognizing the open shoulders of the offensive tackle, the 9 technique should make a direct line to the back shoulder of the quarterback, effectively turning the corner. The offensive tackle will be left in a chase position with no leverage to protect the quarterback. Such a technique described above is called a speed rush.

Should the tackle be disciplined in his pass protection technique and slide outward on the snap of the football, the tackle will be in a better position to block the speed rush. Against this tactic, the 9 technique should again continue to his point of decision, three-yards deep. As the 9-technique end drives upfield, he should lower or dip his inside shoulder. Dipping the shoulder offers the offensive tackle less of a blocking surface. The 9 technique should uppercut punch his inside arm to rip through the tackle's grasp or contact. Once the 9 technique gains upfield leverage on the midline of the offensive tackle, he should point his outside foot toward the quarterback and complete the rip past the tackle. The tackle may keep contact, but he will be left on the hip of the 9 technique as the defensive end turns the corner.

Should the offensive tackle initiate contact and maintain proper protection leverage as the 9 technique works upfield, the 9 technique has another option. If the 9 technique is being walled out from turning the corner, the 9 technique may plant his inside foot and punch his inside arm through the chest of the blocker. The offensive tackle will shift his weight to his upfield foot to counter the punch of the inside arm. As the defensive end plants his inside foot, he bucket steps with the outside foot and spins under the offensive tackle. The outside arm and head of the defensive end whip to enable him to regain sight of the quarterback. The spin move is an excellent recovery move and should be used at a point which the 9 technique is being carried past the quarterback.

Other tactics include the bull rush and the inside move. The bull rush requires the skill of a dominating type of defensive end. The inside move is a good move to make when the offensive tackle commits and extends toward the initial outward steps of the defensive end. The offensive tackle may overextend to a point at which the 9 technique may dip and rip underneath but regain and maintain outside leverage on the quarterback. A key coaching point in regaining outside quarterback leverage is the placement of the outside foot as the defensive end rips underneath.

The defensive end should point his outside foot upfield as his outside leg drives underneath the tackle. Pointing the foot straight upfield will guarantee the recovery of outside leverage on the quarterback.

Not to be neglected is the grab, pull and uppercut punch coaching point of the inside move. As the outside foot is planted, the inside arm grabs the inside arm of the tackle. The grab is made in a fashion similar to a roundhouse punch. Grabbing the tackle's arm near the biceps in the manner of a roundhouse punch adds to the power of the punch. The grab is similar to the widely known slap technique. However, the grab enables the 9 technique to force the tackle to shift his weight to the outer portion of his body. This shift results in lift of the inside portion of the tackle's body and a momentary loss of balance. As the offensive tackle is knocked off-balance, the 9 technique makes the under move by ripping the outside arm under the inside armpit of the tackle. The ripping movement of the outside arm to the inside armpit guarantees clearance for the defensive end.

The final pass rush move available to the defensive end is the swim move. Swim moves may be made inside or outside. The execution of the swim move is somewhat dependent on the relative height difference between the blocker and pass rusher. For this reason, the swim move is not used as much as the speed rush, bull rush, or under move. The defensive player must generally be taller than the blocker for the successful execution of a swim move.

The defensive end makes the swim move when he reaches the three-yard mark and squares up to the offensive tackle. The defensive end will have his buttocks perpendicular to the sideline at this stage of the move. At this moment, the defensive end makes either an inside or outside swim move.

The swim is an excellent pass rushing move. However, to effectively execute the swim move, the pass rusher must have a hitch in his upfield push. The swim move demands a fast push upfield and a momentary stop to snatch and grab the lateral portion of the blocker's upper body near the armpits and shoulders. This momentary stop is not a complete cessation of movement, rather it is a setting point for the pull of the jersey in the swim move.

Both arms will snatch the jersey of the blocker as the defender's hips sink. The pass rusher uses the upfield (outside) arm to pull the pass protector's shoulder downward. The pass rusher jerks the protector's shoulder toward the opposite knee of the pass protector, across the body of the protector.

As the shoulder is pulled downward by the snatch, the 9 technique's downfield (inside) knee drives to a point behind the outside foot of the tackle. At that moment, the swimming arm is swung over the depressed shoulder of the protector in a swimming movement. The key to an effective move is the inside foot of the defender being placed immediately behind the pass protector's outside foot (foot nearest defender). Thus, the arm opposite the pull is punched over the top while the corresponding foot is planted behind the protector. Punching rather than swimming the arm in a long sweeping movement is a better technique for bringing the hand over the blocker's head. Swimming the arm exposes the upper body of the rusher. Punching allows the arm to drive over the head with the palm facing downward. This technique is superior to swimming the hand over.

Once the swing foot is planted in a heel-to-heel relationship with the protector's foot, the swim move is complete. The pass protector has no chance to recover.

One error of a typical swim maneuver attempt occurs when the rusher pulls the protector's shoulder and punches the opposite arm over the head. The novice will not follow through with the foot corresponding to the arm swim. In other words, the left end may jerk the right tackle's right shoulder downward and, punch the right arm over correctly, but fail to swing the right foot to a position immediately behind the blocker's right foot. The protector may recover if the right foot is not swung to a point behind the blocker's right foot.

Another common error when using a swim move is the failure to jerk the outside shoulder of the tackle downward prior to swimming the inside arm over the head of the tackle. Failure to depress the tackle's shoulder with an overhead swim gives the tackle an ideal blocking surface. The tackle will respond by pinning the 9 technique's arm by placing a hand under the armpit. Once the tackle pins the swim arm as it is brought over the tackle's head, the tackle has defeated the swim move of the 9 technique end. The outside shoulder of the tackle must be depressed by the outside arm before the inside arm is punched over the head of the tackle.

The swim move is becoming a less frequently used pass rushing move due to several factors. Teams are placing taller athletes at the tackles as the emphasis on the passing game continues to expand. These tall athletes possess greater reach and are well-coached on keeping their arms extended into the pass rusher. By having taller tackles with an extended reach, the offensive line coach is driving the swim move toward extinction.

Tackles are able to use their reach to prevent the pass rusher from grabbing the shoulder area of the blocker. The swim move is most effective when used by a player who is taller than the pass protector. Few defensive ends, however, are taller than the opposing tackle in the current personnel selection philosophy of most passing teams. Furthermore, when the intricacy of the swim move and the limitations of practice time are also considered, a coach can easily see why the speed rush, bull rush, and the under move are becoming the predominant pass rushing techniques.

STRONGSIDE DEFENSIVE TACKLE

In the 4-3 defense, the strongside defensive tackle alignment is a 3 technique. Although the pre-snap key of the defensive tackle is the ball movement, the 3 technique is also focused on the action of the offensive guard. The 3 technique reads the guard for proper defensive reaction, but keys the ball for movement. Like the other three down linemen of the 4-3, the defensive tackle reads on the run.

The 3 technique's priority is to maintain outside leverage on the guard. He should avoid getting hooked. To successfully defeat the hook block, the 3 technique should attack the outside V of the guard's neck while keeping the outside leg and arm free. The most important factor to defeating a hook block is to get off on the snap of the ball. Exploding into the outside portion of the guard's neck on the snap of the football will guarantee success against the hook block.

Another scheme which attempts to seal the 3 technique inside is the double-team block by the guard and tackle. An additional priority of the 3 technique is to anchor and split the double team. Splitting a double team is accomplished by attacking the post blocker. In the guard and tackle double team of a 3 technique, the post-blocker is the guard. The tackle is the lead blocker. Defeating the past-blocker is the first step in defeating a double team. For a brief instance, the focus of the 3 technique is the guard. The 3 technique attacks the guard just as he would on any base block.

The second step is the dip to the hip reaction of the defensive lineman. As the 3 technique reads the double team of the tackle, the 3 technique should dip the outside shoulder. The shoulder dip is best described as an inward twist of the upper body. The 3 technique twists his torso to the inside as he collapses his outside knee. Dipping the shoulder reduces the blocking surface area available to the defensive tackle. The offensive tackle will usually react to the loss of available blocking surface by swinging his hips outside in an attempt to obtain movement on the 3 technique. Once the tackle adjusts to the shoulder dip by swinging his hips outside, the 3 technique has gained the upper hand and effectively split the double team.

The goal of the 3 technique against a double team is to get his outside hip on the ground before the double team achieves movement. The inward torso twist, the collapse of the outside knee and the outside hip on the ground are critical components to the 3 technique's dip to the hip technique.

Once the 3 technique has dipped to the hip, he drives his legs to drive a wedge through the double team. Merely dropping to the ground is not enough. The 3 technique must attempt to split the double team. Leg drive is the third step in defeating the double team block.

The wall block or the base turn-out block attempts to take advantage of the outside leverage of the 3-technique alignment. The 3 technique defeats the wall block by attacking the guard on the snap of the football and keeping his shoulders square. The 3 technique should fit snugly with the offensive guard and use his arms to create separation and throw the guard. Ideally, the 3 technique squeezes the wall block and closes the A gap with the body of the guard. Squeezing allows the 3 technique to keep outside leverage in his responsible gap while closing the A gap.

In some cases, the 3 technique may cross the face of the guard and come across the wall block. The decision to do this is based upon the same factors which were discussed with the 9 technique. Versus the guard down block, the reaction of the 3 technique is the same as the 9 technique's reaction to the tight end's down block. When the down block occurs, he should expect a trapper. Just as the 9 technique comes under the kick out block, the 3 technique comes under all trap blocks using the wrong shoulder technique. The guard-trap blocking schemes happen very quickly. The tackle-trap blocking scheme take a little longer. Either way, the 3 technique attacks the trapper with the proper technique. Similar to the 9 technique, the follow-through phase of the wrong shoulder technique is essential. The direct running lane through the A gap bubble that a middle trap play is designed to create must be denied.

When the guard pulls across the ball, the 3 technique will chase the play. A preferred technique is for the 3 technique to get in the hip pocket of the pulling guard. The 3 technique should flatten his path down the line of scrimmage as he chases the guard. In getting in to the chase position, the 3 technique dips his inside shoulder and twists his upper body outward. For example, the left 3 technique will dip his right shoulder and twist his body toward his left, depressing his right shoulder. The dip and twist of the upper body help the 3 technique minimize the blocking surface area for the center's fill block. When a guard pulls across the ball, the center will fill for the guard by blocking back toward the 3 technique. Some coaching philosophies call for the defensive tackle to cross the face of the center and pursue down the line of scrimmage. The 4-3 defensive tackle plays the center's block by dipping and going over the top to get in the hip pocket of the guard.

A comprehensive game plan must also dictate the correct response to the guard pulling outside. The 4-3 uses one of two response styles to the tackle-down block and the onside pull of the guard. One response available to the 3 technique is to play the tackle down block over the top and chase by getting in the hip pocket of the guard. The coaching points of this reaction are identical to playing over the top of a center's block—the near shoulder dips to lessen the blocking surface.

Versus certain teams, the 3 technique cannot pursue outside when the guard pulls outside. Wing-T teams are an example of this situation. In this scenario, the outside pull of the guard could mean trap or "gut" plays are coming inside the 3 technique. As a result, when playing against teams that use such an "influence pull," the 3 technique should react just as if the guard had blocked down.

The responsibilities of the 3 technique on pass plays must also be clearly delineated. The defensive tackle should rush the passer and push the middle so that the quarterback will feel as if he should step outside. The 3 technique should rush with at least one hand up. If a 3 technique jumps to block a pass, he should leap upward so that he lands in the same spot from which he leapt.

When engaging a pass blocker, the defensive tackle should use the rip technique. The rip technique is a technique sometimes referred to as the speed rush, particularly when the technique is used by a defensive end. The rip technique is a technique in which the defensive tackle will dip his shoulder nearest the guard as he powers past the guard. The pass rusher uses his leverage arm (the arm closest to the guard) in the manner of an uppercut to the armpit of the pass blocker. This uppercut punch will drive the pass protector's leverage arm upward and force him to open his shoulders and provide a gate to the quarterback. In addition, dipping the leverage shoulder gives the pass protector less blocking surface for contact. The guard's inside arm really has no available frontal surface to contact. The guard has to try to "hip steer" the pass rusher with his lateral arm. The hip steering technique is a technique where the protector puts his off hand on the hip of the speed rusher. It is an effective technique on the edge but not in the interior. The interior defensive lineman has the advantage of a direct line to the quarterback on dropback pass action.

The 3 technique pushes the middle with his free arm up to distract the quarterback. Once the defensive tackle is free of contact with the pass protector, the defensive tackle should rush with both arms extended.

The quarterback should always be sacked with a draping technique. Draping entails bringing both arms down on the shoulders of the quarterback as contact is made. The defensive tackle should sack the quarterback with his arms above the plane of the quarterback's shoulders. The outside arm should reach around the quarterback to hook the elbow of the passing arm as the quarterback cocks his arm in the throwing movement.

The downward hack of the draping technique also helps the pass rusher finish the sack on the agile quarterback who ducks under the pass rusher. By being under control and draping the quarterback, the defender is able to smother the "duck" move by the quarterback. The drape technique helps the tackle finish the sack and keeps him from continuing his forward momentum past the quarterback's duck move.

WEAKSIDE DEFENSIVE TACKLE

The weakside defensive tackle's base alignment is a weak shade on the center. The primary key of the weakside tackle is the ball movement. The weakside tackle also keys the action of the center and/or the weak guard.

The base alignment and scheme response of the 1 technique weakside can best be described as a 3 technique on the center. The 1 technique weak tackle reactions to the schemes are identical to the reactions of the 3 technique tackle.

The primary responsibility of the weakside tackle is to maintain outside leverage on the center. He should never get hooked. The wide shade of the 1 technique weakside helps to guarantee the center will not hook the tackle. A wall block by the center calls for the tackle to squeeze the center or come across the center's face. The correct response is dependent upon the angle of the center's block and the domination factor of the defensive tackle. The center and guard double team is played in exactly the same manner as the 3 technique play of a guard and tackle double team. The trap is also played in the same manner as a 3 technique. The tackle wrong shoulders the trapper and "bubbles" the play.

Should the center hard zone block to the strongside, the defensive tackle must use his hands to flatten the path of the center. Flattening the path of the center accomplishes two things. First, the tackle removes his body from the guard, making it harder for the guard to reach him. Secondly, by flattening the path of the center, the tackle keeps the center from zoning sharply to the second level and cutting off the weakside linebacker.

If the center zones weakside, the defensive tackle jams the center with his inside arm and works down the line of scrimmage. Usually the weakside guard will attempt to rub through the 1 technique's outside shoulder as the center zones weakside. The defensive tackle should use his outside arm to stab the guard and knock him wider. As the tackle stabs the guard, the tackle works laterally into the guard's rub block. This action denies the guard a clean angle to the Mike linebacker and stretches the area which the center must zone. The role of the 1 technique weakside versus the pass is to rush the quarterback and collapse the pocket. The pass rush coaching points are identical for the 1 technique weakside and the 3 technique strongside.

WEAKSIDE DEFENSIVE END

The weakside defensive end plays a 5 technique. The 5-technique end uses the same coaching points in recognizing and attacking blocking schemes as the 9 technique uses. The only difference is that the 9 technique keys the block of the tight end and the 5 technique keys the block of the offensive tackle. The 5-technique end attacks the kick-out block with his outside shoulder and forces the play to "bubble". If the offensive tackle attempts to wall or base-out the 5-technique end, the defender squeezes the block while keeping his shoulders parallel to the line of scrimmage. The 5-technique end may cross the face of a wall block if he is able to make the tackle in the B gap. If the tackle attempts to hook block the 5 technique, the defensive end keeps his outside arm free and fights to maintain outside leverage as he works upfield.

A 5 technique is one man tighter to the ball than the 9 technique. As a result, a 5 technique must be particularly sensitive to the mechanics of the speed rush in order to maintain containment. The 5 technique must widen on pass pro recognition just as he would widen from the 9 technique versus a tackle pass pro read. Conversely, the 5 technique has an advantage over the 9 technique alignment against the pass because of the greater chance of the offensive tackle allowing a lane to develop underneath. The 5 technique also has a slight advantage in bull rushing past the tackle. The shorter edge of the line also gives the 5 technique the advantage in having a shorter path to the quarterback. Offensive tackles tend to open their shoulders when pass protecting against the 5 technique. Any turn of the shoulders of the offensive tackle gives the defensive pass rusher an advantage. (Note: additional details on the pass rushing techniques available to the defensive end are discussed in the section on 9-technique pass rushing.)

The defensive end should tackle the quarterback high. We want the draping type of tackle, except the draping technique is not as exaggerated at the defensive end position. If rushing from the defensive right, the end will gain the high ground and aim for the upfield shoulder. As he initiates the sack, the right arm will chop down on the throwing arm of the quarterback. If the quarterback is attempting to throw, the right arm will hook the elbow of the throwing arm. As the forearm of the defensive end contacts the throwing arm, the defensive end slides his arm down the arm of the quarterback to knock the ball loose.

The chop goes for the elbow because if the end chops for the ball and misses, the defensive end will contact nothing but the air behind the quarterback. The tomahawk to the elbow is a violent hack finished by a jerk toward the ball hand of the quarterback. The ball almost always is successfully stripped when the quarterback's arm is caught in the throwing motion.

If the quarterback catches sight of the defensive end, he will usually bring the ball down to his side in a loose tuck or an extension away from his body. By targeting the elbow, the chop is tight enough to the body to hook the extended arm with the chopping arm. Once this hand grasps the throwing arm in this scenario, the defensive end will pull the passing arm toward him. This action will force the ball arm back and the ball will cock outward from the body of the quarterback. Once the ball is not secured, a prompt arrival of the defensive tackle will result in the unexposed ball being knocked loose from the quarterback's grasp.

If the quarterback manages to tuck the ball, the chop arm will be wrapped around the side of the quarterback. The defensive end will attempt to pull the ball from the quarterback as the sack is completed.

The left hand of the right-side pass rusher (i.e., his off hand), will swing as in a roundhouse punch in an attempt to corral the quarterback's ability to step up. The off arm is the tackling arm. The defensive end secures contact with the quarterback with his off arm. The off arm is swung at chest level of the quarterback. If the quarterback attempts to duck, the defensive end's off arm will grasp the headgear of the ducking quarterback, pressing the quarterback's head down, so that he may not escape. A key coaching point is to teach the defensive end to keep his off hand open. If he grasps the headgear of the ducking quarterback, he may come in contact with the quarterback's facemask.

DEFENSIVE LINE STUNTS

Pinch

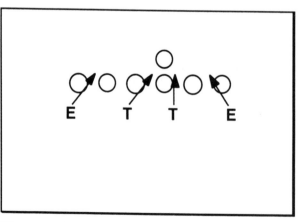

Diagram 4-2.
Pinch stunt.

A "pinch" call tells the defensive linemen to slant inside. The 9 technique attacks the "C" gap while reading the hip of the offensive tackle. The 3 technique attacks the "A" gap while reading the hip of the center. The 1 technique attacks the "A" gap straight ahead. The 5-technique end attacks the "B" gap on the snap while reading the hip of the guard.

The slanting ends and the 3 technique must react on the run to the action of the inside offensive lineman. If the offensive lineman's hip disappears, the slanting lineman should pick up the next threat as he squares his shoulders. If the face of the offensive lineman appears, the slanting defender must knock the blocker to his knees and stuff the gap with the blocker's body. The slanting defender must throw his hands and snap his hips forward as he penetrates the gap. In order to successfully penetrate, the slanting defender should dip his outside shoulder and uppercut his outside arm to help clear the blocker on which he is aligned.

Knife

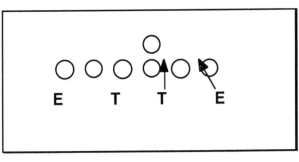

Diagram 4-3.
Knife stunt.

A "knife" call tells the defensive linemen to one side to slant. If the call is made to the right, the right tackle and the end adjacent to him run a pinch. If the call is made to the left, the left defensive tackle and the end next to him run a pinch.

Go

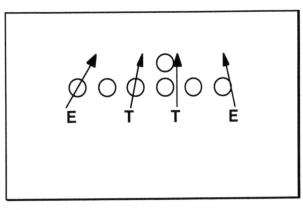

Diagram 4-4.
Go stunt.

The "go" call tells the defensive linemen to execute a speed rush technique through their responsible gap. The linemen play pass first and run second on a "go" call. In addition, the defensive linemen widen their initial alignments.

Cross

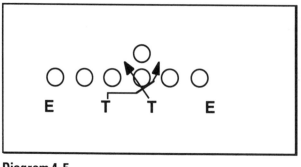

Diagram 4-5.
Cross stunt.

A "cross" call tells the defensive tackles to execute a cross charge. The 1-technique weak attacks the strongside of the center using a slant technique, similar to a 3-technique pinch. The strongside tackle playing the 3 technique stabs the guard and dropsteps his inside foot and drops his outside shoulder as he goes behind the 1 technique move. The 3 technique attacks the weakside "A" gap with his shoulders square.

Tex

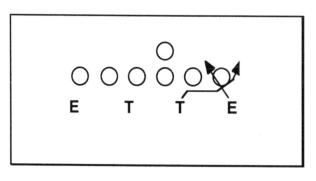

Diagram 4-6.
Tex stunt.

The "tex" stunt is run only to the weakside. The weakside end runs a pinch inside. The 1 technique widens his alignment slightly and jabs his inside foot and dropsteps his outside foot as he loops behind the defensive end pinch. The tackle runs the stunt close off the hip of the end with his shoulders square. The tackle has outside pass rush containment on a tex stunt.

ALIGNMENTS AND RESPONSIBILITIES

The strength of the formation is called "right" or "left" by the position of the tight end. If the formation has two tight ends, the strength is called per the team's game-plan strategy. Certain alignments and techniques will change versus two tight ends. All defensive linemen align on the shade of a man so they can "read" as they "penetrate."

Strongside Defensive End
- Alignment: 9 technique on the tight end.

- Responsibility: *vs. the run*—off-tackle. Coaching points: key the technique of the tight end. Do not get hooked by the tight end. Squeeze all wall blocks by the tight end. Versus the tight end down block, turn inside and look for an outside back or a lineman kick-out threat. Attack the kick-off blocker with the off arm and bubble play.

  vs. the pass—aggressive contain rush.

Strongside Defensive Tackle
- Alignment: 3 technique on the guard.

- Responsibility: *vs. the run*—B gap. Coaching points: key the technique of the guard. Do not get hooked by the guard. Squeeze or come across the wall block by the guard. Turn out on a guard-tackle double-team block and try to split it. Versus a guard down block, turn inside and attack the trapper with the off arm and bubble play. Versus a guard pull backside, chase. Versus a guard pull onside, use strategy per the game plan.

  vs. the pass—rush the quarterback; collapse the pocket.

Weakside Defensive Tackle
- Alignment: I technique on the center (Note: his alignment may vary according to the offensive formation or the line-stunt call)

- Responsibility: *vs. the run*—A gap. Coaching points: key the technique of the center and/or the weakside guard. Do not get hooked by the center. Squeeze or come across a wall block by the center. Turnout on a center-guard double-team block and try to split it. Versus a center backside block, turn inside and attack the trapper with the off arm and bubble play. Versus a center pull backside, chase. Versus a center pull onside, use strategy per the game plan.

  vs. the pass—rush the quarterback; collapse the pocket.

Weakside Defensive Tackle

- Alignment: 6 technique on the offensive tackle.

- Responsibility: *vs. the run*—off-tackle. Coaching points: key the technique of the offensive tackle. Read the block of the offensive tackle. Do not get hooked by the offensive tackle. Squeeze all wall blocks by the offensive tackle. Versus an offensive tackle down block, turn inside and look for the onside back or a lineman kick-out threat. Attack the kick-out threat with the off-arm and bubble play.

    vs. the pass—aggressive contain rush.

CHAPTER 5

Linebackers

ALIGNMENTS

Key:

Razor linebacker—the right outside linebacker

Mike linebacker—the middle linebacker

Lazor linebacker—the left outside linebacker

Lazor always plays on the left side of the formation and Razor always plays on the right side of the formation.

POSITION	ALIGNMENT	KEY
Mike linebacker	0 technique on center	Fullback
Razor and Lazor linebackers	Versus the tight end: 7 technique on the tight end	Tight end and tackle to backfield flow
	Versus open-end side: 5 technique on the offensive tackle	Tackle and guard to backfield flow

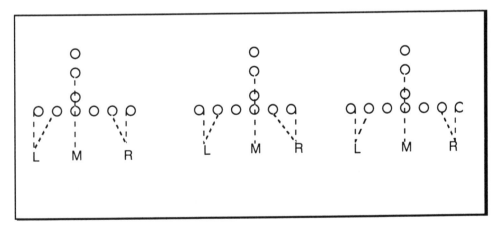

Diagram 5-1.

In Diagram 5-1, all linebackers are aligned five yards off the line of scrimmage.

RAZOR AND LAZOR LINEBACKER READS AND REACTIONS

The Razor and Lazor linebackers each key two adjacent linemen. The linebacker on the tight end side keys the tight end and the offensive tackle. The linebacker on the open side keys the offensive tackle and offensive guard. The initial read will be the offensive linemen that the linebacker is shaded on followed by the next offensive linemen to the inside. Some reaction will occur during the initial read as shown in the following diagrams.

Razor/Lazor Linebacker "Flow To" Reactions

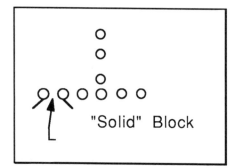

Diagram 5-2.
Tight end blocks out; tackle blocks inside (solid block). Charge L.O.S. and attack lead blocker with inside shoulder.

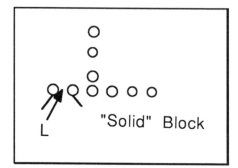

Diagram 5-3.
Tackle blocks out; guard blocks inside (solid block). Charge L.O.S. and attack lead blocker with inside shoulder.

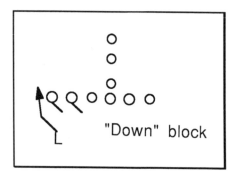

Diagram 5-4.
Tight end blocks inside on L.O.S. (down block). Replace outside hip of tight end, play spill-out on L.O.S.

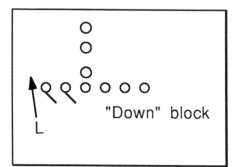

Diagram 5-5.
Tackle blocks inside on L.O.S. (down block). Replace outside hip of tackle; play spill-out on L.O.S.

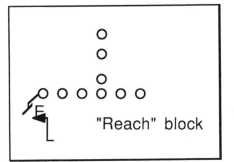

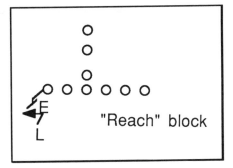

Diagram 5-6.
Tight end hook/ reach technique
(reach block). Step up, check "C" gap;
play inside-out to ball.

Diagram 5-7.
Tackle hook/reach technique (reach
block). Step up, check "B" gap; play
inside-out to ball.

Razor/Lazor Linebacker "Pull Away" Reactions

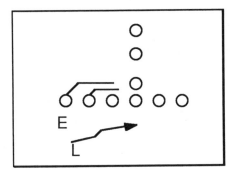

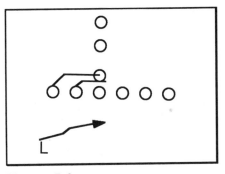

Diagram 5-8.
Tight end pulls away. Check onside
"A" gap; run to ball (inside-out)
looking for cutback.

Diagram 5-9.
Tackle pulls away. Check onside "A"
gap; run to ball (inside-out) looking for
cutback.

Razor/Lazor Linebacker "Base-Flow To" Reactions

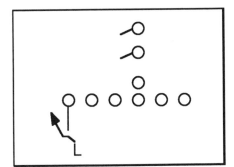

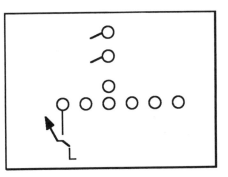

Diagram 5-10.
Tight end base block. "Rock-step" out
(read looks like down block). Key to
backfield flow to; replace outside hip
of tight end; play spill-out on L.O.S.

Diagram 5-11.
Tackle base block. "Rock-step" out
(read looks like down block). Key
backfield flow to; replace outside hip
of tight end; play spill-out on L.O.S.

Razor/Lazor Linebacker "Base-Flow Away" Reactions

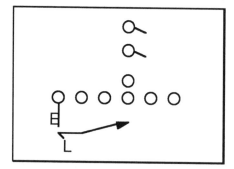

Diagram 5-12.
Tight end base cut-off block. "Rock-step" out (read looks like down block). Key backfield flow away.

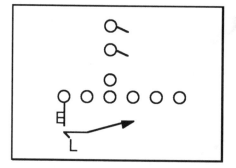

Diagram 5-13.
Tackle base cut-off block "Rock-step" out (read looks like down block). Key backfield flow away.

MIKE LINEBACKER READS AND REACTIONS

The Mike linebacker can shade the center slightly to the tight end side to get a better view of the fullback. He keys the fullback and makes a short lateral step, then checks the guard to the side of the fullback movement. If the guard is pulling away from the fullback, the Mike linebacker goes with the guard, playing inside-out to the ball. If the guard does anything else as a run blocker, the Mike linebacker continues his charge to the fullback. If the guard shows pass, the Mike linebacker goes to his pass responsibility.

The Mike Linebacker also has to recognize the "closed window." This situation occurs when one of the defensive linemen, while reading and reacting properly, closes off the hole to which the fullback and the Mike linebacker are going. In this case, the Mike linebacker veers out to the adjacent gap. This action should always happen on trap plays.

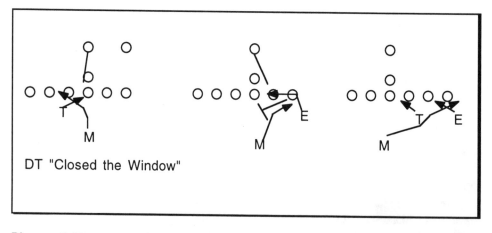

DT "Closed the Window"

Diagram 5-14.

CHAPTER 6

Secondary Coverages

Cover 4 is the base coverage scheme for the 4-3 defense. The actual huddle call for our coverage will be Cover 41, 42, or 43. The defense plays Cover 4 versus standard formations with two opposite wide outs and two backs (i.e., pro formation). The second number in the coverage call designates the coverage to be played versus formations with two or more wide outs on the same side (i.e., trips, or twins). Cover 4 is used with our basic front. The basic front play is aggressive and upfield. An aggressive pass rush is important because the cornerbacks are playing the wide receivers man-to-man, perhaps with some help from the half safeties (depending on the type of run/pass read the safeties get.) Cover 4 enables the defense to get nine men quickly to the run as well as good pass rush pressure to make sure the cornerbacks do not have to cover for long periods of time. Cover 4 can be disguised with late movement by the cornerbacks in and out of "press" alignment and, also, with late movement by the safeties in and out of two-deep or three-deep pre-snap look alignments.

BASIC COVER 4 ASSIGNMENTS

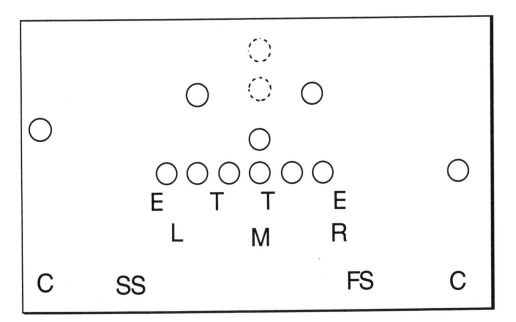

Diagram 6-1.

Cornerback Responsibilities: Versus the Pass

In Cover 4, the cornerbacks are playing their wide receiver (#1 receiver) man-to-man. The cornerback is aligned in either an inside-shade backpeddle position (from five to seven yards deep depending on the speed of the receiver) or in a "heavy" bump-and-run pressed alignment. A "heavy" bump-and-run pressed alignment is a squared-up position shaded slightly inside that makes it difficult for the receiver to release straight upfield. This alignment is naturally a little more vulnerable to the inside release than the man under two-deep alignment in which the cornerback prevents an inside release with a definite inside alignment and knows he has deep help from the half safety.

In Cover 4, the cornerback cannot assume that he will have any deep help. The cornerback attempts to get a quick "pop" on the receiver with his inside hand to stop his upfield release and then attempts to maintain his inside position on all patterns. He must learn to read patterns and receivers' eyes, and how to attack the receiver intelligently. The other choice is standard inside-shaded backpeddle coverage, which is a little safer on deep patterns, but not as good on short out or hitch patterns. The defense can mix in a "cross over" backpeddle technique that will help us on "out" patterns. This technique originally looks like a standard inside shade backpeddle alignment, but at the snap of the ball, the cornerback quickly backpeddles to an outside position to give him a better attack angle on out patterns.

Cornerback Responsibilities: Versus the Run

In Cover 4, the cornerbacks only play run if their wide out crack blocks on a wide run. In that case, the cornerback calls "crack" and replaces the man being crack blocked. In pressed alignment he should be able to stop the crack block. He should be alert for pre-snap crack block clues, such as short splits by the receiver or motion down the line, and warn the player in danger of being cracked. Because he is in man coverage, the cornerback must chase reverses across the field while calling "reverse."

Quarter Safeties Responsibilities: Versus the Pass

The quarter safety of the single receiver side helps the cornerback with inside patterns and, if possible, deep patterns. His basic alignment is eight yards deep and on the outside shade of where the tight end normally would line up. On passing downs, a wider, deeper alignment is possible.

The quarter safety on the two-receiver side has the same alignment as the single-side quarter safety. However, he must read the tight end (or the #2 receiver). If the tight end pass blocks, the quarter safety is free to help on the #1 wide out on inside or deep patterns. If the tight end drags or runs out to the flat area, the quarter safety can again concentrate on helping the cornerback on the #1 receiver. If the tight end runs a vertical pass route. The quarter safety should focus on taking out the deep part of the pattern, since the linebackers will not chase the receiver deep. Because the quarter safeties read run first, they may be late reacting to the deep half when a good play-action fake is given in a running situation or if the tight end blocks on passing plays.

Quarter Safety Responsibility: Versus the Run
The quarter safeties are basically responsible for wide runs and cutbacks. In agreement with the principle of inside-out pursuit developed by Tom Landry in his design of the 4-3 front, the basic defense will "spill" many running plays outside, and the quarter safeties should be there to make the tackle. Safeties away from the running play must become the extra man in charge of stopping the cutback. The linebackers are running recklessly to the ball and are vulnerable to cutback and reverse maneuvers. Defending the reverse is also part of the backside quarter safety's job. He should look to the wide receiver on the side of a wide run away from him and check for the reverse. The Cornerback will also be chasing the reverse.

COVER 4—Underneath Coverage
Our underneath coverage is unlike traditional zone coverages where linebackers drop to designated zones and cover anybody who comes into their zone. The coverage is also unlike traditional man coverages that assign certain inside receivers to inside linebackers. However, the coverage has strong similarities to both.

First, the three inside linebackers are not to be concerned with wide receivers. The wide receivers are covered by the cornerbacks who are often helped by the safeties. The inside linebackers are in a match-up zone with three inside receivers. (Note: Versus a twins or trips formation we check out of Cover 4 and our coverage assignments become more traditional.)

The Lazor and Razor linebackers drop slightly lateral to an approximate depth of eight yards. As soon as one of the inside receivers becomes the #2 receiver in the pattern, the Lazor or the Razor linebacker locks on him man-for-man and stays with him.

The Mike linebacker drops to the side of the tight end or to the side of flow for about a depth of eight yards. As soon as one of the inside receivers becomes the #3 receiver in the pass pattern, the Mike linebacker locks on him man-to-man and stays with him wherever he goes.

Diagrams 6-2 to 6-4 illustrate several sample pass routes and the appropriate underneath reaction.

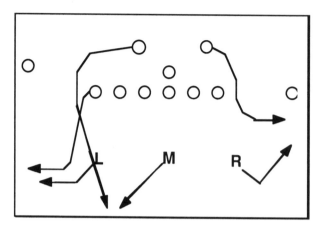

Diagram 6-2.

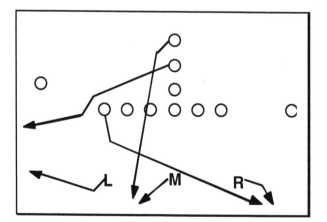

Diagram 6-3.

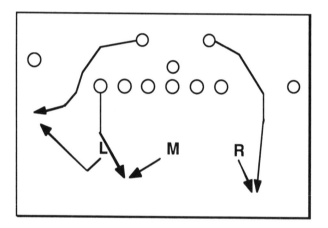

Diagram 6-4.

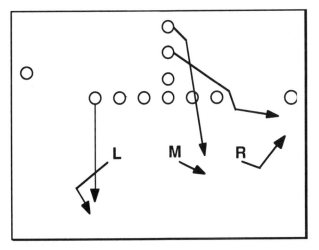

Diagram 6-5.

Note: If the #2 receiver releases straight upfield on a vertical route, one of the safeties will be helping on the top of the pattern.

COVER 2

Cover 2 is played when the coverage call is "42," and two wide receivers are aligned to one side. In Cover 42, the secondary coverage will be Cover 2 against a twins or trips set.

The strong safety will declare to the two-receiver side and play his normal position on the inside receiver. The strongside cornerback will roll up to the hard-corner position on the outside receiver. The free safety will move to the half safety on the two-receiver side, while the weakside cornerback plays the other half safety. This coverage alignment provides the defense with a 3-on-2 numerical advantage to the two-receiver side. To the nub side of the formation, Cover 2 offers a sound look with the outside linebacker and the weakside cornerback. The base alignment for Cover 2 is illustrated in Diagram 6-6. The suggested field of vision afforded a cornerback in a Cover 2 is shown in Diagram 6-7.

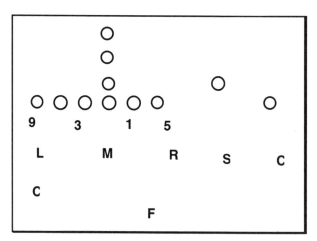

Diagram 6-6.
Base of Cover 2 alignment.

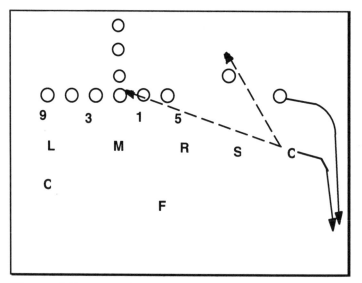

Diagram 6-7.
The cornerback's field of vision in Cover 2.

The Strongside Cornerback in Cover 2

The strongside cornerback in Cover 2 plays the hard corner position. The hard-corner provides an overlapping run force as the running play spills outward to him. Versus the dropback pass, the hard corner jams the outside receiver with outside leverage and reads through him to the inside receivers and ball. On run flow away, the hard corner guards against the throw-back pass to the split end and rotates slowly to the middle as if in a madcap man-to-man responsibility on the split end. Once no possibility exists of a pass from the run flow away from the cornerback, the hard corner takes a cutoff angle to prevent the breakaway touchdown down the opposite sideline.

The strongside cornerback in Cover 2 plays what is called the "settle" technique. In this technique, the cornerback will read through the receiver to the ball and settle on any outside threat to the flat.

The base alignment of the cornerback will vary according to situation. Versus a short to intermediate distance at the appropriate down, the cornerback may align at the press position. Versus a down and distance situation where the offense needs longer yardage, the cornerback may align as deep as seven yards off the widest receiver. Normal alignment for a hard corner is usually four yards off the receiver and one yard outside. A hard corner never aligns closer than four yards to the sideline.

The hard corner looks inward and presnap keys the ball and the quarterback. He may be slightly cocked inward, but also may be aligned with his shoulders square, depending on philosophy. Many coaches align the more athletic cornerback square to the line of scrimmage when playing the hard-corner position. The philosophy of our 4-3 defense is to play the cornerback in the squared-off position and to step to gain outside leverage versus a pass read.

On the snap of the football, if pass is read and the receiver approaches, the squared-off cornerback takes a lateral step and delivers a two-hand open-hand blow to the receiver's chest. The hips must be kept low so the cornerback will not get knocked off balance. The hard corner attempts to keep the upfield leverage (stay slightly in front) on the receiver during the jam. The cornerback jams the receiver to accomplish four things. First, the corner wants to force the receiver to take an inside path. Second, the corner wants to disrupt the route and consequently the timing of the pattern. Third, the corner wants to send a physical message to the receiver and disrupt his concentration. Fourth, the corner wants to flatten the outside release of a receiver forcing the receiver to turn his shoulders to the sideline.

If the receiver takes a flat and exaggerated inside release, the corner should close with him (but not more than three steps) and immediately throw his eyes inside to pick up the inside threat to the flat. A flat release against Cover 2 is indicative of a split-end post-corner route. The corner should release off the inside squeeze and sink off and gain width while searching out the inside-receiver route.

If the split end takes an exaggerated outside release, the corner should move laterally and flatten the release. A forced outside release is indicative of a possibility of two verticals in the half. On the outside release, the corner jams and snaps the eyes back over the inside shoulder to find the number two receiver or other flat threat. The outside ride of the receiver should last not more than two to three yards. The hard corner should always visualize a transversal line across the field which runs about five to seven yards behind the line of scrimmage. This line is referred to as the rail or line of release. At the normal depth alignment, the corner should reach the line of release in three to four steps as he flattens the outside path of the receiver. Once the corner rides the receiver to the line of release, he must make a decision on the presence of a threat to the flat. If no flat threat exists (i.e., the Z receiver on the twins has not broken to the flat), the corner may do one of two things.

Since Cover 2 in a 4-3 defense is a coverage used against twins, the Cover 2 hard-corner reaction to a wide release is to play with focus on the threat of the inside-receiver threat. The corner will attempt to get his chest into the inside shoulder of the receiver and execute a speed turn inside once he reaches the line of release. This action would enable the corner to see the quarterback more clearly and recognize the threat of a receiver in the flat. Once the corner squares, he speed turns inside and cushions under the outside receiver if no threat to the flat is recognized. This technique is a common technique for the high school and college hard corner. It is best when executed from the softer alignment, five to seven yards off the receiver. Tighter alignments, as in the man-under-two-deep coverages, are used for a more focused technique on the outside receiver. The base Cover 4 is a man-under-two-deep concept, but the Cover 2 scheme in the 4-3 adheres to the pure zone, eyes never leave the quarterback, speed turn inside, type of coverage from the hard corner.

The corner's area of responsibility is to a depth of 15 yards down the sideline. Any inside receiver threat to the sideline within 15 yards is his responsibility. It is important to note the corner looks for any inside receiver threat to his zone. This means he should look across the field as he speed turns inside to cushion the area under the wide receiver. If a receiver is dragging across the field, the corner must release, settle and move to meet the receiver.

Versus the run block of the wide receiver and the run flow to the corner, the corner must get his hands on the pads and throw him to the inside. The corner should maintain outside leverage and squeeze the running lane while keeping his shoulders parallel to the line of scrimmage. The 4-3 hard corner's responsibility is secondary containment. He should never attempt to cross the face of a receiver unless the receiver has position blocked him. A wide receiver who swings his buttocks inside to position block the corner may be beaten over the top. Attempting to go under the receiver's position block may result in the corner being pinned inside. If the receiver attempts to cut the corner, the corner should get his hands on the receiver's helmet and push the receiver's head to the ground as he maintains proper leverage.

Against the sprint-out movement toward the corner, the corner gains width and settles. Against the sprint out movement away from him, the corner cushions the outside receiver in a man-to-man coverage technique to the inner boundary of the outside $1/3$ of the field, approximately four yards outside the hash.

Diagrams 6-8 through 6-10 illustrate the cornerback's reaction to three different passing situations.

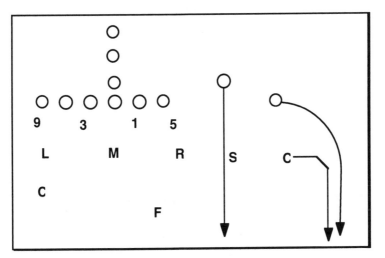

Diagram 6-8.
Cornerback's reaction to #2 receiver on a vertical route in Cover 2.

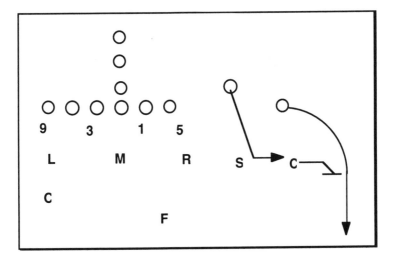

Diagram 6-9.
Cornerback's reaction to #2 receiver on an out route in Cover 2.

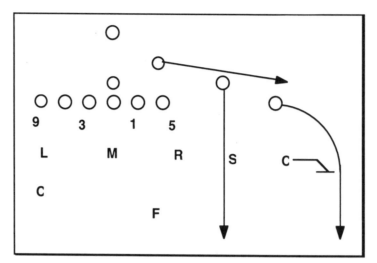

Diagram 6-10
The cornerbacks reaction to #3 receiver on a flat route in combination with #2 receiver on a vertical route in Cover 2.

The Free Safety Half Zone Technique

The free safety will play half the field in Cover 2. The free safety backpedals on the snap and moves to reach a point 25 yards deep near the hashmark on pass recognition. The read is the quarterback and the number two receiver. The half-field coverage free safety first reads ball movement through the quarterback. If pass is read, the free safety reads through the number two receiver—the Z on twins.

If number two releases outside, the free safety must widen and get over the top to cover the number one receiver. The free safety doesn't lose sight of number one when widening. If number one is falling upfield on a skinny post as the number two receiver releases outside, the free safety cannot overrun to meet the number one threat. The free safety must be able to cover number one over the top, but maintain a proper relationship in his half zone—particularly with the threat of number one to break his route skinny or vertical into the near half. If number one digs or curls, then the free safety has more leverage to overplay number two on the outside release. If number one crosses the field, the free safety looks to pick up the action of number two as he gains depth.

If the quarterback sprints to the side of the half safety, the safety weaves outward to the sideline as he picks up the wide threat. If the quarterback rolls out away from the free safety, the safety weaves inward to the middle of the field.

Versus the run toward the safety, the safety checks the release of number one. If number one is releasing down the sideline, the safety overlaps just as he would on the sprint-out pass. The free safety is a pass defender first. If the number one receiver releases inside, the free safety searches the eyes of the receiver. An inside release is usually indicative of a play-action pass. The free safety picks up the number one on the play action threat. If number one is attempting to block the corner, the free safety moves to overlap the strong safety and replace the corner. This action provides a fail-safe measure for secondary containment. The free safety is responsible for the alley between the strong safety and the sideline. Should the corner be sealed outside, the free safety will replace him and provide a tackling containment. Should the corner defeat the block of the wide receiver and close the alley, the free safety reads the alley door as closed and continues to move to a position of second containment on the outside hip of the corner.

Versus the run away from the safety, the half safety is an alley filler. He should make the hit if the ballcarrier cuts back or hits the crease in the alley. As the ball moves down the line, the free safety mirrors the ball. Once the run read is guaranteed, the free safety drives to fill the alley.

The Half Cornerback in Cover 2

The cornerback opposite the twins or trips plays on the nub end (i.e., the tight end side). His alignment is at a 10-12 yard depth over the offensive tackle. His coaching points are the same as for the free safety half position in Cover 2. His luxury is having only one receiver to his side, and the one receiver is tight. The close proximity of the tight receiver to the ball would normally allow the cornerback to play more of a relaxed zone. The tight end cannot horizontally stretch the half zone as a wide receiver split can stretch the zone.

Versus a tight side of a formation, a half-secondary technique player should key the ball and then immediately seek out number one. Since the zone is a type of squat zone to the twins side, the responsibility of covering the tight-side flat and out is given to the outside linebacker. Naturally, the tight end has an advantage in getting open in the flat quickly due to the linebacker's primary responsibility of reading run first. A play-action pass can freeze the outside linebacker as the tight end releases on an arc release. The tight side cornerback must understand the dynamics of the linebacker duties and key hard on the tight end after the ball is snapped.

The corner should backpedal outside as the key is read. An outside backpedal will put the corner in a position to cover the tight end over the top should he take an arc release for a banana route outside with a play-action fake at the outside linebacker. The half-technique corner coverage on the tight side is close to a man-to-man principle. The corner should be keenly aware of the placement of a nearback on the tight side. A common combination pattern to attack the Cover 2 tight side is the tight-end vertical to a skinny post, coupled with the nearback on a wheel down the sideline. The corner must be able to provide over the top help for the outside linebacker on this combination route, as well as maintain a proper relationship on the tight end. An outside-weave backpedal is critical to sound half corner play in this coverage.

Run responsibilities are also the same for each half-zone technique player. The reader should refer to the previous discussion on the half-zone free safety technique for more information on playing half zone technique.

The Strong Safety in Cover 2

The strong safety technique in Cover 2 is similar to the strong safety technique in Cover 3. In Cover 2, the strong safety is not flat responsible, nor does he jump an outside release of an inside receiver. The hard corner assumes that responsibility in Cover 2. He should rob the curl versus a sprint-out pass toward him. Against a sprint-out pass away from him, he should look for a screen back to his side, then move to rob the middle of the field, providing underneath coverage on the backside post and robbing the backside crossing route. The 4-3 strong safety should deny an inside release of the slot receiver. In essence, the strong safety plays man-to-man on an inside release of the slot receiver, with sprint out away from him.

The stance of the strong safety from the invert or the sky position in Cover 2 is a balanced stance. In Cover 3, the strong safety should have a slightly staggered stance with his outside foot back as he looks over his inside shoulder to the ball. Should the coach want the same stance at all times, the Cover 3 stance is an acceptable stance for the Cover 2 coverage.

In Cover 2 versus the pass, the strong safety should sink his hips and jam his hands into the numbers on the receiver's jersey. The strong safety will disrupt the vertical route and cover the receiver in the vertical alley. The strong safety should attempt to knock the vertical-releasing receiver inside to the outside linebacker, while staying on the upfield shoulder and looking in to the quarterback. While the strong safety is responsible for an underneath zone, a vertical route by number two demands the strong safety provide a cushion coverage on the vertical number two. If number two releases outside, the strong safety sinks and robs the curl area. If number two takes an exaggerated flat release inside, the strong safety closes two steps inside and looks through for an inside receiver flaring across his face and reads the quarterback's eyes for a slant route behind him by the wide receiver. If number two releases on either a direct angle or a delayed break off a vertical, the strong safety cushions off the break and yells "out, out, out" to alert the cornerback. Once the out break is made, the strong safety searches out the number one route and settles. If number one is on an inbreak, the strong safety picks him up. If number one is on a vertical route to 15 yards, the strong safety sinks and peeks across the field for a drag. If no drag is coming out of the tight end, and a third receiver is not attempting to slip into the onside seam, the strong safety can then work to width and help the cornerback, particularly for the double outs from the split end and the slot receiver.

Versus the number two receiver attempting to block him, the strong safety attacks the receiver and uses his hands to gain separation, while keeping his shoulders square to the line of scrimmage. The strong safety is the primary force, meaning he is responsible for closing the alley and forcing the ball to turn in. In Cover 2, the strong safety has the cornerback outside of him providing secondary containment. This fact allows the strong safety to attack the perimeter more recklessly in Cover 2 and to push the edge deeper, thereby forcing a deeper "bubble" should the ball break the force containment of the strong safety.

Cover 2 Underneath Coverage
When the defense checks to Cover 2, the linebackers then know that they will play pass plays with traditional zone drops. If facing a twins formation, the outside linebacker on the two receiver side drops to the curl zone approximately twelve yards deep in the vicinity of the hash marks. The linebacker should have his head on a swivel as he looks at the quarterback and then back to the wide receiver. Once the ball is thrown, he breaks to the ball wherever it is. The outside linebacker on the weak side drops curl-to-flat. Once he gets to the curl zone, if no threat occurs, he proceeds to the flat zone. He also keeps his head on a swivel and breaks on the ball. The middle linebacker drops to the hook zone on the tight-end side using traditional zone-drop techniques.

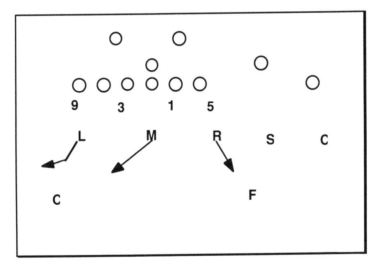

Diagram 6-11.

If defending a trips formation with a check into Cover 2, the assignments are the same except that the middle linebacker now drops to the hook zone to the side that the ace back flows toward.

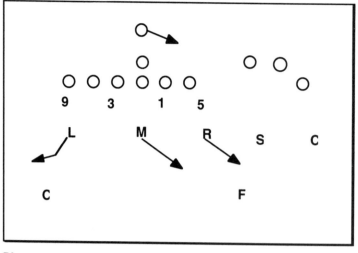

Diagram 6-12.

If the read is a run away from the strong safety, the strong safety shuffles backward with his shoulders square playing the reverse. Once there is no threat of reverse, the strong safety takes an appropriate pursuit angle across the field.

Coverage 42 Variations

Diagrams 6-13 through 6-20 illustrate variations of Coverage 42 that can be employed against specific offensive formations.

Terminology key for Diagrams 6-13 to 6-20:

h-c   Hook to curl
c-f   Curl to flat
$^1/_2$ Halves
Key RB Key the remaining back
⬚ $^1/_5$ Underneath Zone

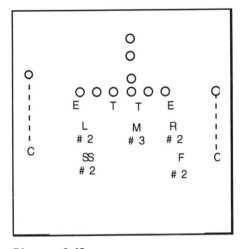

Diagram 6-13.
Play Cover 4.
Coverage 42—Variation #1.

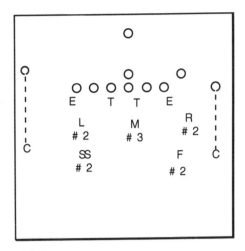

Diagram 6-14.
Play Cover 4.
Coverage 42—Variation #2.

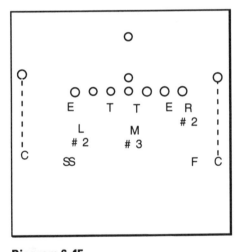

Diagram 6-15.
Play Cover 4.
Coverage 42—Variation #3.

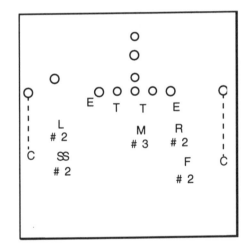

Diagram 6-16.
Play Cover 4.
Coverage 42—Variation #4.

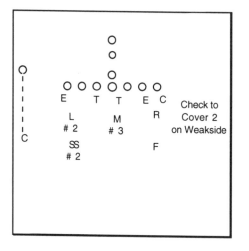

Diagram 6-17.
Play Cover 4 with Cover 2 on Weakside.
Coverage 42—Variation #5.

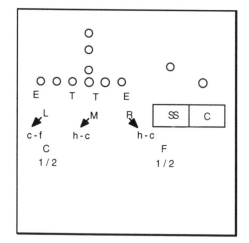

Diagram 6-18.
Play Cover 2.
Coverage 42—Variation #6.

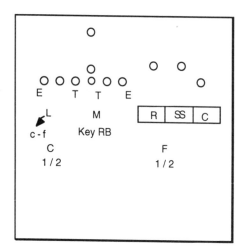

Diagram 6-19.
Play Cover 2.
Coverage 42—Variation #7.

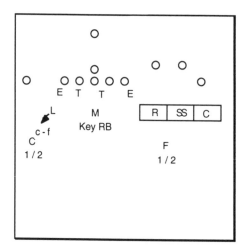

Diagram 6-20.
Play Cover 2.
Coverage 42—Variation #8.

COVER 3

Cover 3 is played when the coverage call is "43," and two wide receivers are aligned to one side. In Cover 43, the secondary coverage will be Cover 3 against a twins or trips set.

Strongside Cornerback Play in Cover 3

The strongside cornerback aligns on the outside receiver to the two-wide receiver side. His alignment may vary according to down and distance and according to the philosophy of coverage. The 4-3 Cover 3 scheme against a twins formation is a 2-on-2 coverage situation. Most 2-on-2 coverage situations in Cover 3 call for a tighter cornerback alignment. However, as mentioned, the depth is also dependent upon the down and distance and the game situation.

The base alignment of the deep $1/3$ responsible cornerback is five yards off the receiver and one yard outside. He never aligns closer than six yards from the sideline. The middle of his zone is nine yards from the sideline, or the top of the numbers. If the receiver moves beyond the nine-yard mark, the cornerback deepens his alignment to a depth of seven to nine yards.

The cornerback backpedals on the snap of the ball as he reads the quarterback. In his first three steps, he reads the quarterback drop. If the quarterback mechanics show a quick route, the cornerback sinks his hips and sits down for the stop route or the out route. If the quarterback mechanics show an intermediate route, the cornerback slows his backpedal and gets his eyes to the receiver. If the short or intermediate mechanics are not shown, the corner continues in his backpedal and maintains proper upfield leverage on the receiver. The angle of the backpedal is toward the top of the numbers—the middle of his zone.

The deep $1/3$ corner must turn and run when the alignment cushion is broken. If the receiver streaks down the sideline, the corner should squeeze the receiver's route and press him into the sideline. The corner should execute an inside-speed turn on a sideline vertical and look back over his inside shoulder to the quarterback. This technique places the cornerback in between the ball and the receiver and enables him to help defend the four-vertical receivers pattern.

The deep $1/3$ corner squeezes the post move to the hash, but leaks through the post move to pick up the inside receiver wheel. Against the post-corner, the corner should speed turn back outside and break under the receiver, again playing between the ball and the receiver. The corner plays the inside moves over the top, remaining on the upfield and outside shoulder of the receiver. Playing the post move underneath will cause the corner to be burned on the post-corner and the post-vertical.

Versus sprint out toward the corner, the corner should weave to the sideline and overplay the sideline. Versus sprint out away from the corner, the corner should match up on the receiver in a man-to-man technique.

Versus run flow toward the corner, the corner plays pass first. If the receiver stalk blocks him, the corner strikes him face up with outside leverage and throws him to the inside. A quick inside dip-and-rip move with the outside arm and shoulder across the receiver is available to the corner if he is positive he can make the move cleanly. Once the corner makes the inside move, the corner must regain outside leverage of the ballcarrier. The corner should not run around the block unless the receiver over positions himself to the inside. The corner should attempt to keep his shoulders square as he provides secondary containment to the strong safety. Versus run flow away from the corner, the corner plays as he would against sprint-out pass flow away.

Free Safety Play in Cover 3
The free safety is responsible for the middle $1/3$ of the field. The free safety assumes a relaxed stance typical of a deep-coverage technique player. The alignment is over the middle of the formation. A twins or trips formation will face a free safety alignment over the guard to the receiver strength. The presnap key is the quarterback through the uncovered lineman. The uncovered lineman will provide a sharp and consistent run-pass key against teams which fake the ball well. If the ball is moving through a run fake but the uncovered lineman is popping up, the read is pass. The weak side guard and the tackle will usually provide the most consistent uncovered reads in the 4-3 alignment.

The free safety should backpedal to an approximate depth of 18 yards. The normal alignment for a free safety is 12 yards from the line of scrimmage. Upon recognition of a dropback pass, the free safety should check the twins side for a threat to the middle. The free safety should always look through the route of the slot to the wide receiver. An outside break of the number two receiver from the twins is indicative of a possible post route out of the number one.

The free safety should swivel his vision back to the nub side, particularly on recognition of no threat from the twins and a nearback set on the tight side. A nearback set on the tight side is a set which supports the wheel combination and the tight end on a skinny post. Key coaching points include gaining depth as long as the quarterback holds the ball, providing inside-out alley pursuit to the either side, and weaving with the ball movement to a square location over the ball while reading the quarterback's shoulders and eyes.

The Weakside Corner in Cover 3
The weakside corner in Cover 3 aligns five yards off the line of scrimmage and three yards outside the tight end. He keys through the tight end to the ball. On the snap of the ball, the corner backpedals slowly while reading through the tight end for a run

or pass key. The tight end will provide a more accurate run-pass key, since he is the only threat to the deep zone on that side of the formation. A corner who overlooks the tight end and keys into the backfield and the quarterback may get burned on a play action fake toward the corner. The weakside corner should angle his backpedal slightly outside as he reads the tight end.

If the tight end releases, the corner maintains outside leverage on him as the corner looks through to the inside and the ball. The corner squeezes the route of the tight end until a threat attempts to cross his face from the inside. The corner should be aware of the location of the nearback. A back near the tight end is a threat to cross the face of the corner as he squeezes a vertical route of the tight end. The corner should not jump the route of the out-breaking tight end in the flat until the ball is thrown. The outside linebacker is flat responsible. The corner, however, may realize the run-stopping responsibility of the linebacker on the play-action fake and cover the tight end more closely on a release with a play-action fake at the outside linebacker.

If the tight end drags shallow and no threat appears from the backfield, the corner should cushion to his zone and look across the field for a crossing route. The cornerback must never chase the tight end if he drags. The corner may squeeze the tight-end post as long as no inside receiver is attempting to cross his face.

Versus run flow with the tight end base blocking or blocking inside, the cornerback chops his backpedal and drives up at an angle to squeeze the alley. The cornerback is the primary force provider on a run toward him. Versus option flow with the tight end arc blocking, the corner maintains outside leverage on the tight end, but does not commit to the line of scrimmage until the ball is pitched or the quarterback reaches the tackle box.

Versus run flow away from the corner, the corner settles and keys hard on the tight end. If the tight end is blocking, the corner settles and plays reverse. If the tight end releases inside, the corner mirrors his inside movement in a man-to-man technique. Once the ball reaches the line of scrimmage on the opposite side, the corner pursues at the proper angle to cut off the ballcarrier.

The Strong Safety in Cover 3
The strong safety aligns on the outside shoulder of the inside receiver of the twins formation. However, the strong safety should not align more than 10 yards from the tackle. The strong safety must take care to align so he can provide force support and the wide run toward him. Unlike Cover 2, Cover 3 does not provide for a hard corner outside the strong safety. The loss of outside leverage when squeezing the alley from Cover 3 would allow the ballcarrier to get around the edge to the sideline. The strong safety keys and his initial movement in both Cover 2 and Cover 3 are the same—the ball through the backfield and shuffle two steps out and back on the snap.

Another difference between Cover 2 and Cover 3 strong safety play is the reaction to a vertical route out of the inside receiver. The strong safety will settle and disrupt the route in both coverages. However, the strong safety will not cushion under the number two vertical in Cover 3. He will work his way out to the flat through the curl zone as he sneaks a peek at the split end. Also, the Cover 3 strong safety will roll to the flat on a sprint-out pass toward him. The Cover 2 strong safety technique is to settle on sprint out toward him.

Versus run away from him, the Cover 3 strong safety will shuffle backward and close with his shoulders parallel as he looks for reverse. Once the reverse is not a threat, the strong safety rotates to the middle and takes a proper pursuit angle. Versus run toward him, the strong safety plays his normal force technique, maintaining outside leverage and closing the alley without excessive penetration into the backfield.

Cover 3—Underneath Coverage

The underneath coverage in Cover 3 is similar to Cover 2, in that the linebackers utilize traditional zone pass drops. Versus twins formation, the assignments for the linebackers are identical to their assignments in Cover 2. One outside linebacker goes to the curl zone; the other linebacker goes to the curl-to-flat zone; and the middle linebacker goes to the tight-end side hook zone. When defending a trips formation, the assignments are the same with the exception that the middle linebacker in Cover 2 drops to the hook zone on the side of the Ace back movement. In Cover 3, however, he must drop to the hook zone on the side of trips receivers.

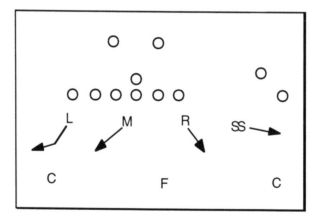

Diagram 6-21.
Cover 3 vs. twins formation.

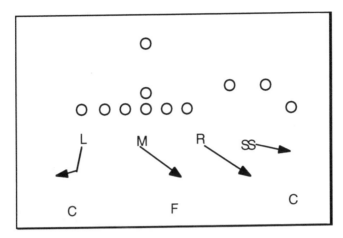

Diagram 6-22.
Play Cover 4.
Coverage 43—Variation #2.

Coverage 43 Variations

Diagrams 6-23 through 6-30 illustrate variations of coverage 43 that can be employed against specific offensive formations.

Terminology key:

h-c   Hook to curl

c-f   Curl to flat

$^{1}/_{2}$ Halves

Key RB Key the remaining back

☐ $^{1}/_{5}$ Underneath Zone

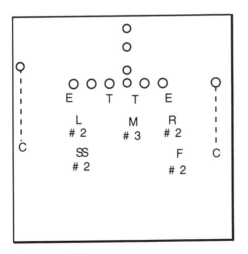

Diagram 6-23.
Play Cover 4.
Coverage 43—Variation #1.

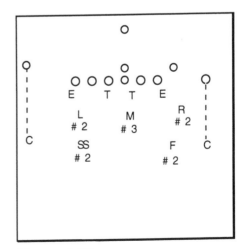

Diagram 6-24.
Play Cover 4.
Coverage 43—Variation #2.

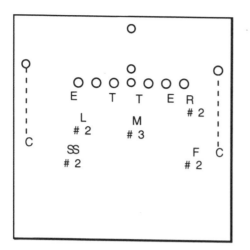

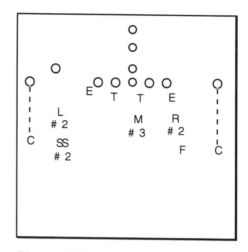

Diagram 6-25.
Play Cover 4.
Coverage 43—Variation #3.

Diagram 6-26
Play Cover 4.
Coverage 43—Variation #4.

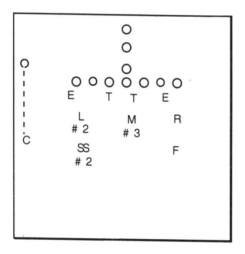

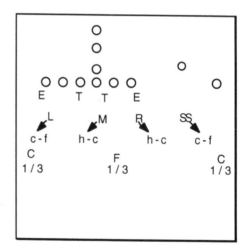

Diagram 6-27.
Play Cover 4 (with weakside Cover 2).
Coverage 43—Variation #5.

Diagram 6-28.
Play Cover 3.
Coverage 43—Variation #6.

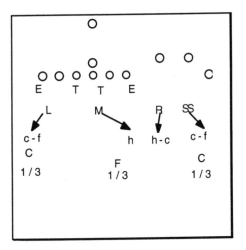

Diagram 6-29.
Play Cover 3.
Coverage 43—Variation #7.

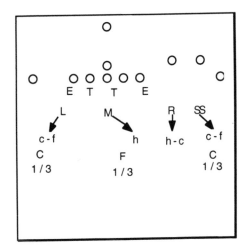

Diagram 6-30.
Play Cover 3.
Coverage 43—Variation #8.

CHAPTER 7

Basic Blitz Package

The 4-3 defensive alignment offers numerous possible blitz combinations. A team, however, can be effective using only three blitz schemes. Limiting the number of schemes used enables a team to use just one coverage for all blitzes. Furthermore, the three blitzes complement each other in the way they attack the line of scrimmage gaps. Both blitzes are necessary as change-ups to the basic reads, and they both put significant pressure on the offensive blocking assignments.

The blitz coverage is called Cover 0. The cornerbacks cover the #1 receivers man-to-man. The safeties cover the #2 receivers man-to-man. If the formation has three receivers on one side, the off-side safety will shift over and cover the #3 receiver.

"DOG" BLITZ

Huddle call: Dog Cover 0

In a "dog" blitz (Diagram 7-1), the defensive ends are in a go charge. They have what is called a "green" assignment, in which they rush upfield. If a back crosses their face to the outside, they instead attack and cover him.

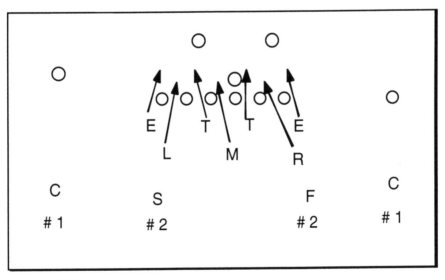

Diagram 7-1.

"FIRE" BLITZ

Huddle call: Fire Cover 0

In a "fire" blitz (Diagram 7-2), the defensive linemen execute a pinch line stunt. The Razor and Lazer walk up to a spot on the line of scrimmage just outside the defensive ends. On the snap of the ball, they charge across the line of scrimmage into the offensive backfield. Versus most teams, Razor and Lazer will go under all blocks except pass blocks. The Mike linebacker is responsible for the release of the #3 receiver to either side. Versus a trips formation, the Mike linebacker is man-to-man with the Ace back (Diagram 7-3).

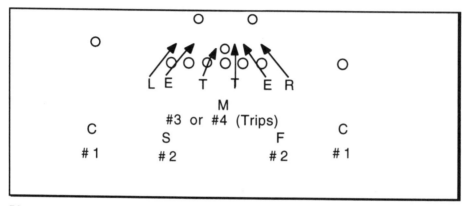

Diagram 7-2.

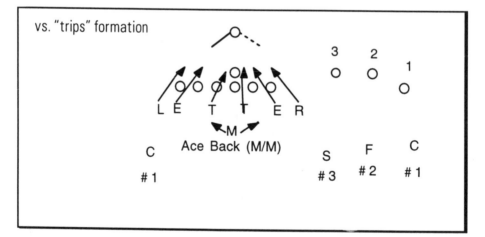

Diagram 7-3.

"FIRE SWITCH" BLITZ

Huddle Call: Fire Blitz Cover 0

This blitz is identical to the "fire" blitz, except that the ends slant out and the outside linebackers charge across the line of scrimmage inside the ends (Diagram 7-4).

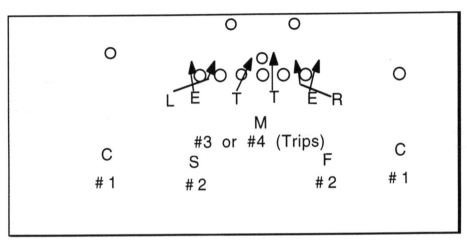

Diagram 7-4.

Addressing Problem Areas

No single defense can be equally strong versus every mode of offensive attack. All defenses have some potential weaknesses that the coach must address. In the 4-3 defense, these problem areas include linebacker bubbles, the vacated weakside linebacker spot, and quarters coverage.

PROBLEM AREA: LINEBACKER BUBBLES

The first problem area a coach using the 4-3 must address relates to the basic structure of the defensive front. This type of 4-3 configuration has three linebacker bubbles. Other defensive alignments have two or fewer linebacker bubbles. Various linebacker bubble configurations are illustrated in Diagrams 8-1 through 8-5.

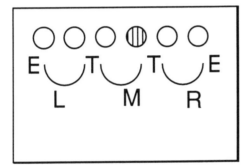

Diagram 8-1.

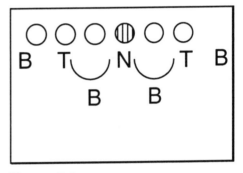

Diagram 8-2.

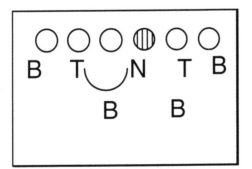

Diagram 8-3.

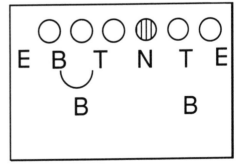

Diagram 8-4.

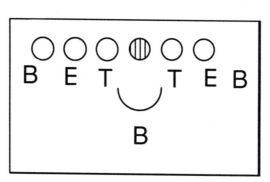

Diagram 8-5.

The presence of three bubbles in the defensive structure results in a softer front than most other defenses. Consequently, most offenses will try to attack the bubbles in several ways. The effectiveness of these attacks can be minimized with a combination of good execution of the basic defense, linebacker blitzes and lineman cross charges, and an occasional use of a change-up defensive front.

Isolation-type plays are one of the primary methods used to attack a 4-3 defense. In these plays, the offense tries to isolate one of the three linebackers (Diagrams 8-6 through 8-8).

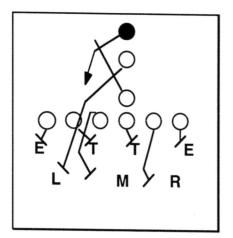

Diagram 8-6.

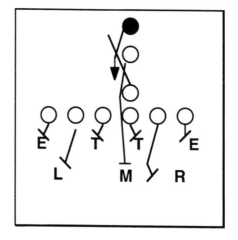

Diagram 8-7.

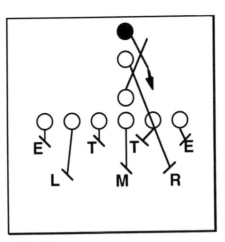

Diagram 8-8.

Another popular method of attacking the bubbles is to use wind back or cutback plays (Diagrams 8-9 and 8-10). Sometimes, these plays are run by design, and sometimes they just happen. Either way, these plays can exploit any vulnerability of the 4-3 defense.

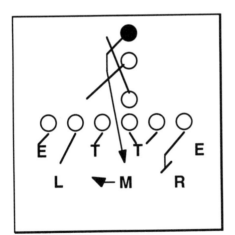

Diagram 8-9.

Diagram 8-10.

Although isolation plays and cutback plays should be a concern to a coach using a 4-3 defense, performing numerous repetitions of this defense properly can minimize the effectiveness of such plays. In defending the isolation play, the Razor or the Lazor linebacker, upon reading the "solid" blocking scheme, should charge forward and meet the isolation blocker at the line of scrimmage. He should take on the block with his inside shoulder, thereby forcing the ball back to the other linebackers who can subsequently beat their blockers with quick, aggressive read-reactions (Diagram 8-11 and 8-12).

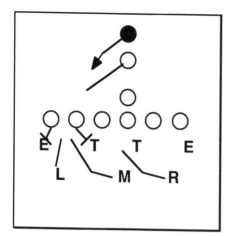

Diagram 8-11.

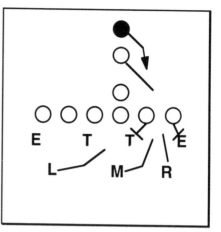

Diagram 8-12.

When the Mike linebacker is isolated, he should take on the isolation blocker with his strongside shoulder, thereby forcing the ball to the tight-end side, where the outside linebacker has a better chance of evading an offensive blocker (Diagram 8-13).

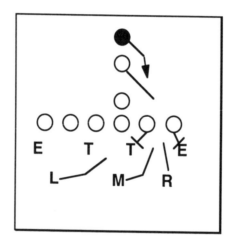

Diagram 8-13.

In defending against a cutback play, it is crucial for the Razor and Lazor linebackers to know that if they get a tackle base block read, coupled with backfield flow away, they should hit the strongside A Gap as hard as they can. That gap is where running backs usually go when they decide to cut back, regardless of whether they started on the strongside or the weakside (Diagram 8-14).

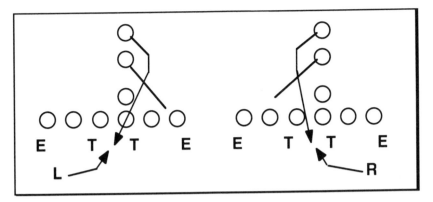

Diagram 8-14.
Cutback usually goes to the tight-end of the A gap.

It is also important that a coach never underestimate the value of the Cover 4 safeties as described in Chapter 5. The backside safety is like an extra linebacker who is looking for cutback or reverse plays.

Even with good coaching and proper execution of this defense, most teams that run this particular 4-3 defense have at least one change-up defensive front that has fewer than three bubbles. These teams also have several linebacker blitz charges in their basic 4-3 defensive scheme that will "flatten" the linebacker bubbles.

Because the change-up defensive front used at Clovis High School resembles the popular Chicago Bears 4-6 alignment, we call it the "Bear" defense. Our team reduces the defensive end on the open-end side and designates one of the outside linebackers to align on the open-end side on the line of scrimmage and to rush. The defensive end on the tight-end side plays an 8 technique, head-up on the tight end, and is required to keep his inside arm free. The weakside defensive tackle aligns over the center. He attacks the center head-on, but favors the gaps away from the tight end. The Mike linebacker aligns on the outside shade of the strongside guard and executes the same "fullback-to-near-guard" read that he does from the 4-3 defense when aligned on the outside shade of the center. The other linebacker aligns on the open-end side and executes his open-end side read/techniques. The defensive alignment now has fewer than three linebacker bubbles. In the "Bear" defense, we play a man-free coverage. The Mike linebacker and the strong safety play a combination coverage versus the tight end and the near back (Diagrams 8-15 and 8-16).

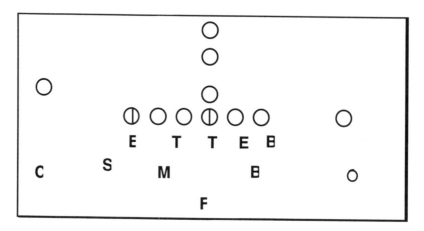

Diagram 8-15.

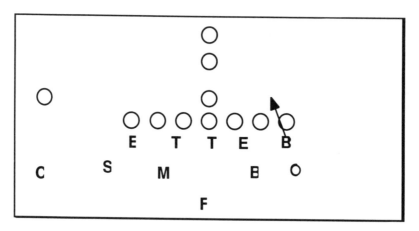

Diagram 8-16.

The "Bear" defense is similar to the very popular University of Arizona "Wildcat" defense. Since it is only used as a change-up defense, however, we do not incorporate all of the blitzes, flexed tackles, and other variations of the "Wildcat" defense. However, the "Bear" defense does use cross charges with the interior defensive linemen. The defensive-line cross charges are the same as those executed from the 4-3 alignment, thereby simplifying things for the defensive linemen (Diagrams 8-17 and 8-18).

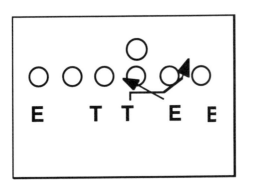

Diagram 8-17.

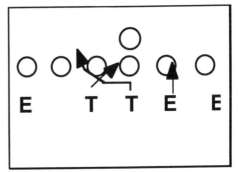

Diagram 8-18.

In summary, the prospect of an opponent consistently and successfully attacking the three bubbles of the 4-3 defense can be greatly minimized with the combination of good execution of the 4-3 defense fundamentals; several linebacker blitzes and lineman cross-charges; and the occasional use of a change-up defensive front.

PROBLEM AREA: VACATED WEAKSIDE LINEBACKER SPOT

Another problem occurs when certain offensive formations cause a team to move linebackers from their normal alignment to alignments near the offensive receivers in the perimeter. The Ace-doubles formation, for example, forces the weakside linebacker to vacate his bubble alignment for a position in the perimeter. This move forces the defense to cover the run with only six defenders in the "tight end/tackle box." Some defensive coaches prefer to always keep seven defenders "in the box." Embracing that philosophy, however, limits the scope of the Cover 4 coverage. Other teams, Clovis High School included, prefer to stay in Cover 4 versus Ace-doubles (Diagram 8-19). However, doing so with the weakside linebacker spot vacated means the Mike linebacker is now responsible for two gaps (Diagram 8-20).

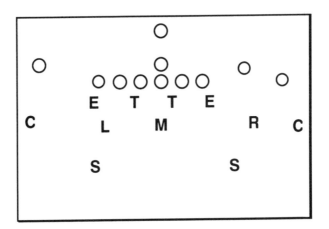

Diagram 8-19.

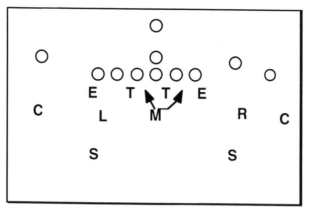

Diagram 8-20.

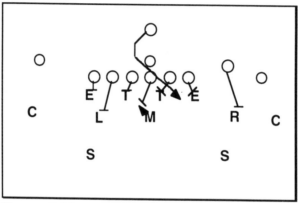

Diagram 8-21.

When the Mike linebacker has two gap responsibilities, the wind back play with a solid block becomes a serious problem (Diagram 8-21). Not only is a situation created where the defense has no Razor linebacker, but the cutback safety cannot help in the same fashion as he did when there were two backs in the backfield. In theory, he is still a "quarters" player with cutback responsibility versus flow away. In reality, however, he is now more of a "halves" player because of the increased threat of the pass in the Ace-doubles formation. The safety must be alert to three particular pass routes: the wheel, the smash, and the vertical (Diagrams 8-22 through 8-24).

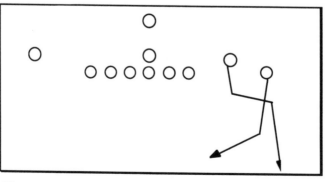

Diagram 8-22.
Wheel pattern.

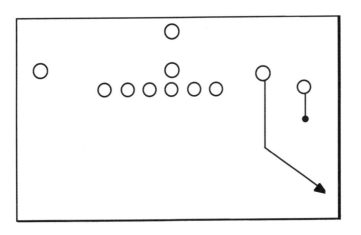

Diagram 8-23.
Smash pattern.

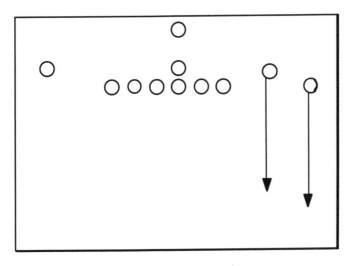

Diagram 8-24.
Vertical pattern.

In all three of these pass routes, the safety is asked to help the outside linebacker with his coverage. Consequently, the safety will widen and deepen his alignment. His role as a run-support defender is significantly decreased. He may still get to his run-support position, but it will be later than normal.

Clovis High School practices two different solutions to the Ace-doubles problem: the "walk" mode and the "seven-in-the-box" mode. To stay in Cover 4 coverage, the outside linebacker is "walked" out to the #2 receiver (i.e., the "walk" mode). In the "walk" mode, the Mike linebacker, instead of shading the tight-end side of the center, now shades the open-end side of the center. He also reminds himself that he is now responsible for two gaps, and that he needs to slow down his flow reaction. His reads, however, are the same (Diagram 8-25).

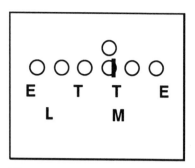

Diagram 8-25.

The outside linebacker who "walks" must call "tex" to the defensive linemen to his side. The linemen then execute a "tex" cross charge at the snap of the ball. This line stunt will help the Mike linebacker in defending the wind back play (Diagram 8-26). If the play works for the offense at all, this adjustment will make it less clean and less direct and will make it easier for the Mike linebacker and the safety to get to the ball.

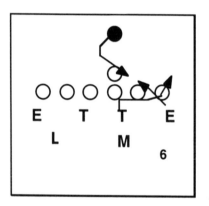

Diagram 8-26.

A second solution is to keep "seven in the box." In this situation, the defense checks out of Cover 4. The weakside safety slides over and covers the #2 receiver man-to-man. He, like the cornerback, has no help in his coverage (Diagram 8-27).

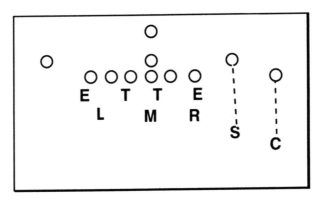

Diagram 8-27.

This solution, by itself, is not complete for two reasons. First, the team has now lost the safety responsible for cutback defense. Second, it is dangerous to play this type of "naked" man-to-man pass coverage without heavy pressure. A blitz can solve both of these problems. A team can execute the "slash" mode, in which both of the outside linebackers are blitzing versus the Ace-doubles formation. As soon as the outside linebacker recognizes the Ace-doubles formation, he tells the defensive linemen on his side to "knife." The defensive end executes an inside charge, while the linebacker blitzes from the outside. The blitz is similar to the "fire" blitz, but only includes the outside linebackers and the defensive ends (Diagram 8-28). It is important that the entire secondary be aware that in the "slash" mode versus an Ace-doubles formation, the team will be in blitz coverage, Cover 0.

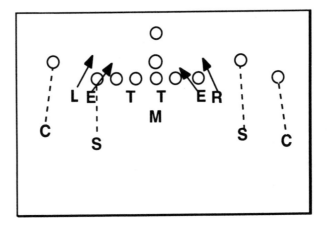

Diagram 8-28.

The "walk" and "slash" modes give a defense two effective solutions to the Ace-doubles formation problem. Against the Ace-trips formation, a team can switch to a Cover 1, 2, or 3. The linebackers do not move out of the box. They must be aware of the coverage change, however, and the fact that no "quarters" safety is behind them. Therefore, they must be more aware of playing the cutback play when the flow goes away (Diagram 8-29).

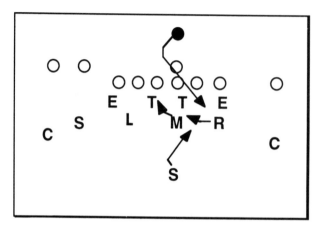

Diagram 8-29.

Clovis High School has a two-platoon football system. This situation means the defensive coaches and players can work together for the entire practice period, an approach which enables the coaches to teach multiple adjustments and solutions to defensive problems. Before each game, the coaches usually condense and simplify the defensive package for that game. For some football programs, one-platoon football teams in particular, finding the time to teach multiple adjustments and solutions is relatively difficult. One simplification that will greatly reduce the amount of teaching necessary is to treat all Ace formations in the same way. A team takes one of the solutions—"walk" or "slash"—and applies it to both Ace-doubles and Ace-trips formations. This approach will eliminate the need for the pass coverage secondary to go from Cover 4 to either Cover 3 or Cover 1 versus Ace-trips. Another simplification that prevents a defensive team from having to check out of Cover 4 versus a twins formation is to bring the cornerback on the side without a wide receiver over to the two-receiver side.

These adjustments give a team a simplified defensive game plan package. For example, if "slash" is the preferred solution, then the coaches can teach the three formation adjustments illustrated in Diagrams 8-30 through 8-32. The defensive huddle call would be Cover 4 slash.

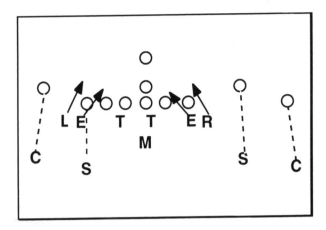

Diagram 8-30.

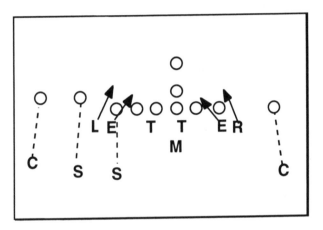

Diagram 8-31.

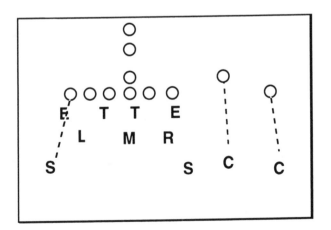

Diagram 8-32.

Whether a team uses the simplified package or a more complex one, one other formation that needs special attention is a two-back formation with no tight end (Diagram 8-33).

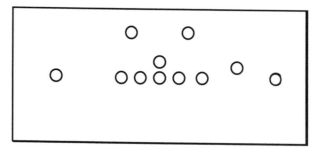

Diagram 8-33.

Each of the cornerbacks must stay on their side; thus a linebacker has to "walk" out to the #2 receiver. This leads to the "six-in-the-box" gap-control problem. The solution is to teach the players to treat a two back with no tight end formation just as they would an Ace formation. This strategy can be justified by citing the number of eligible receivers in the box. If the box has two or fewer, this approach approximates the Ace formation adjustment.

The number and difficulty of the adjustments and the solutions must be determined by each individual coaching staff. However, regardless of the situation or the defense, a complete plan of formation adjustments is an essential part of defensive game plans in modern football.

PROBLEM AREA: CERTAIN PATTERNS VS. QUARTERS COVERAGE

In Cover 4, the cornerbacks are locked onto the wide receivers in man-to-man coverage. Some coaches who use this coverage instruct their cornerbacks to drop off their man and retreat to their deep one-fourth of the field zone versus certain pass routes, namely the shallow crossing route, the hitch route or the hitch and slide route (part of the smash route), and the wheel pass route.

In the following illustrations, the smash and the wheel pass routes are diagrammed in the Ace-doubles formation. These patterns are very effective from this formation. However, many other formations could be used for these same pass routes. The principles of Cover 4 coverage versus these pass routes are the same regardless of the formation (Diagrams 8-34 through 8-36).

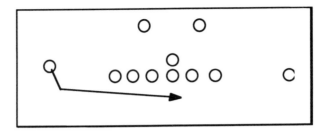

Diagram 8-34.
Shallow crossing pattern.

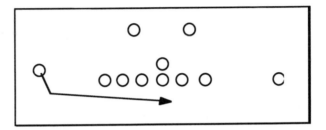

Diagram 8-35.
Smash pattern.

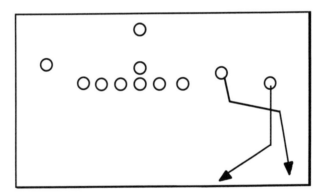

Diagram 8-36.
Wheel pattern.

These problem pass routes can all be handled in the same manner. The safety should be alerted to various formations and potential pass routes. For example, if a linebacker is walked out versus an Ace-doubles formation and the coach wants to stay in Cover 4, the safety should be aware of potential smash and wheel pass routes. The safeties primary responsibility is to help the linebacker (Diagrams 9-37 and 9-38). The cornerback remains locked onto the #1 receiver in man-to-man coverage. The same is true versus the shallow crossing route. The defense can also allow the cornerback to use an inside press bump-and-run technique, in order to deny the shallow crossing release by the receiver. This method is an often-used variation to Cover 4.

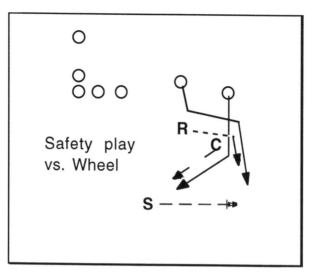

Diagram 8-37.
Safety vs. wheel play.

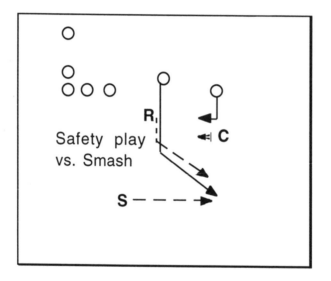

Diagram 8-38.
Safety vs. wheel pattern.

In Clovis High's version of Cover 4, the cornerbacks maintain their man-to-man technique on all pass routes by their receiver. We are never forced out of this concept. It is important, however, for a defense to have some coverage variations, such as Cover 2 or Cover 3, in every game plan (Diagrams 8-39 and 8-40).

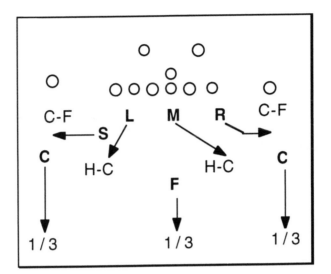

Diagram 8-39.
Basic, Cover 3.

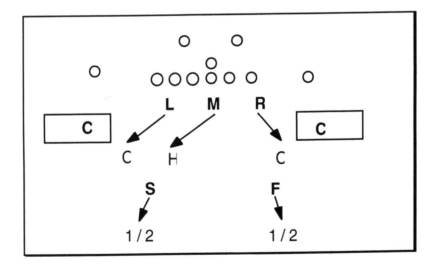

Diagram 8-40.
Basic, Cover 2.

CHAPTER 9

Defending Various Offenses

At Clovis High School, we see three basic categories of offense from our opponents: the Wing-T, the pro style, and the run and shoot. We do not see the wishbone or the split-back veer. In the mid-1980s, the California Interscholastic Federation introduced rule changes which prevented players from blocking below the waist. This rule change had a substantial impact on teams using option systems in which "load" and "junction/arc" techniques included blocking below the waist. However, several teams outside our area still use the wishbone and the split-back veer with great effectiveness.

Because any of the three basic offensive schemes that we have to defend against could include option plays, having a sound option defensive scheme is still very important. We see virtually equal numbers of teams using Wing-T and pro style offenses. As a general rule, we face very few run and shoot teams. These teams, however, are potentially very potent if they have good coaching and talented players.

Regardless of the style of offense we are defending, the principles of the 4-3 defense that have been previously described remain intact. While a good run and shoot team that also employs a triple option does disfigure our basic 4-3 alignment, the fundamentals and the techniques we use are still the same.

VERSUS THE WING-T

The Wing-T is a very popular offense in high school football at the present time. Diagram 9-1 illustrates how the 4-3 defense with Cover 4 can be applied to the base Wing-T formation.

With two minor adaptations, the basic Cover 4 reads and responsibilities will be effective versus a Wing-T attack. Placing four defenders outside the offensive tackle to the tight end/wing side of the formation allows the defense to outnumber the buck sweep play and the down option play. One adaptation is to roll the cornerback up to the line of scrimmage head-up on the wing back. This approach is a common alignment for us on the single tight end side versus a double tight end formation. This alignment enables the defense to attack the onside pulling guard on the buck sweep more quickly and to restrict the free release of the wing back to the outside linebacker (Diagram 9-2).

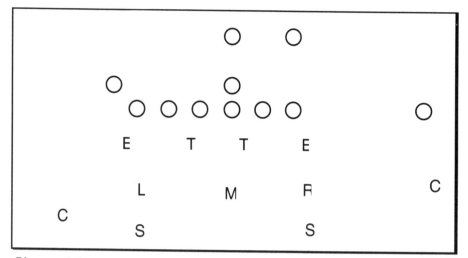

Diagram 9-1.

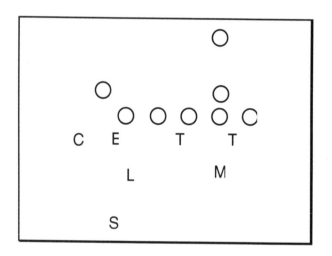

Diagram 9-2.

The defense needs three men outside the tackle on the split-end side to defend the belly option and to cover the split end. The basic alignment has four defenders outside the tackle. This alignment is over-kill, as well as a dangerous mistake versus the Wing-T. If a defense is over-loaded in one area, then it is under-loaded in another. The Wing-T offense is a complete running attack. If the defense is weak somewhere along the line of scrimmage, the Wing-T offense can exploit that weak area with serious consequences. If a team makes no adjustments on the split-end side, four defenders will be outside the tackle and only three defenders inside from tackle to tackle. In this situation, the defense would be very vulnerable to the deceptive, quick hitting, highly efficient inside-running game of the Wing-T attack (Diagram 9-3).

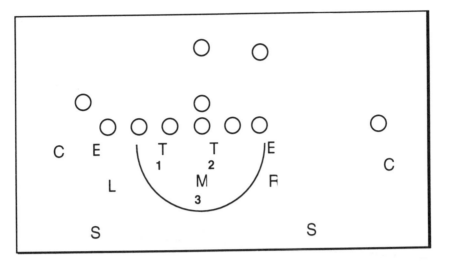

Diagram 9-3.

Thus, the other adaptation versus the base Wing-T formation is to align the split-end side outside linebacker in the B gap. His reads stay the same. It is similar to the way he lines up on a tight-end side and reads the linemen on either side of the gap in which he is aligned (Diagram 9-4). Once this adaption has been made, the team will have the proper number of defenders on the flanks and inside. All of the basic reads and assignments can be executed from this alignment. It is important to remember that the outside linebacker on the open-end side and the cornerback on the tight end/wing side need to be coached on their additional assignments.

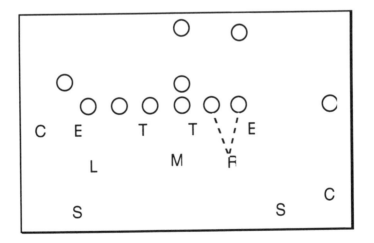

Diagram 9-4.

In this adjustment, the open-end side linebacker should key adjacent linemen as usual, with two exceptions. First, if the guard pulls outside, the linebacker becomes the contain rusher versus the waggle pass. On the waggle pass, the guard will hook the defensive end. Versus the sweep, the linebacker should take the same path and try to make the tackle in the backfield. On the sweep play, the guard will be looking to kick-out the safety. The linebacker should scrape underneath the guard. Second, if the tackle pulls to the inside as he would on a tackle trap, the linebacker should not follow him; he should remain in the area for the tackle-trap pass. The rolled-up cornerback should line up on the line of scrimmage nose-to-nose with the wing back. The cornerback should jam the wing back with his hands and flatten the wing back's inside release. He should then stay on the line of scrimmage and play under all blocks. He must not get kicked out by a guard. Versus the option, the cornerback should wait for whomever shows in his area. It could be the fullback or the quarterback. He should not dive down inside to help on the inside part of the play. If the wing back releases outside, the cornerback should think pass and play any short, outside-pass route.

Diagrams 9-5 through 9-14 illustrate the 4-3 defense against a variety of basic Wing-T plays with the expanded defensive assignments installed.

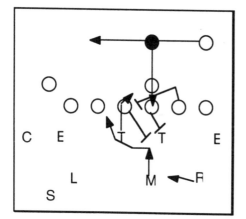

Diagram 9-5.
Buck trap.

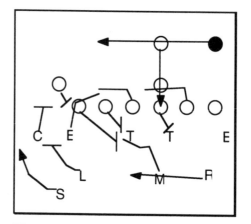

Diagram 9-6.
Buck sweep.

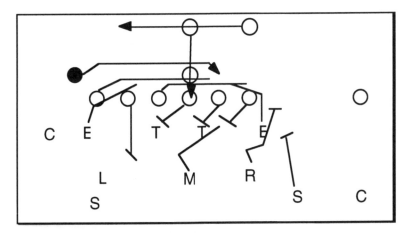

Diagram 9-7.
Wing reverse.

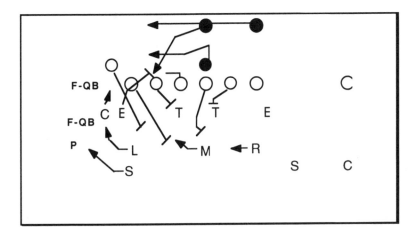

Diagram 9-8.
Down option.

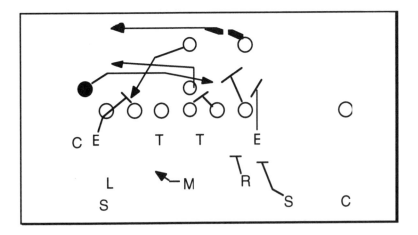

Diagram 9-9.
Wing Sally.

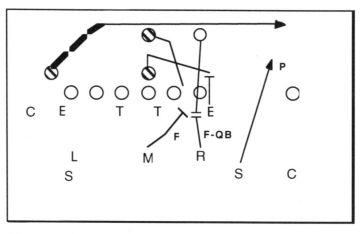

Diagram 9-10.
Belly option.

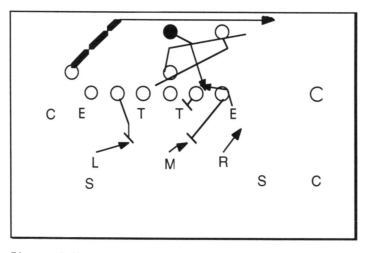

Diagram 9-11.
Over play.

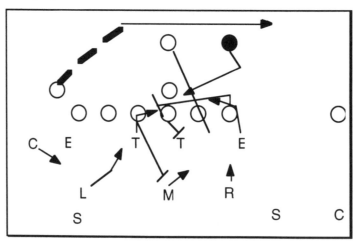

Diagram 9-12.
Tackle trap.

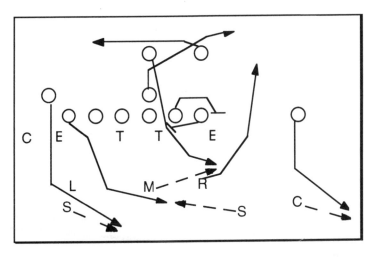

Diagram 9-13.
Waggle pass.

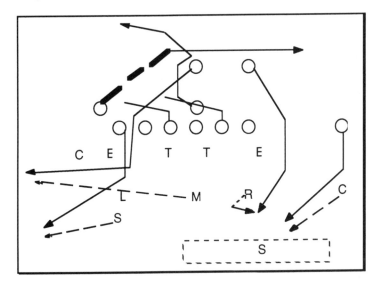

Diagram 9-14.
Wing motion waggle pass.

In summary, defending the Wing-T offense does not call for any major changes from the basic 4-3 defense. The basic coverage can be effective versus the Wing-T's potent running game with only minor adjustments. One area of concern should be the inside running game breaking past the linebacker level. There is no free safety down the middle of the formation to make play-saving tackles. Furthermore, all Wing-T inside plays are accompanied by good faking on each flank. This factor has the effect of "freezing" the safeties in their outside areas. If an inside run breaks clean, it could go for a very long gain. An adjustment that can be made is to pinch the 3 technique defensive tackle on any type of guard pull. This step will strengthen the inside running defense. Also, repetition versus the inside running game in practice is essential.

VERSUS THE PRO STYLE

The pro style offense, when operating at its best, is a very balanced attack. Facing this type of attack, a team must be able to defend the whole field against the pass and the entire line of scrimmage against the run. The two basic blocking techniques used with the pro style offense are zone blocking and gap blocking. Basic zone blocking includes both an inside zone play and an outside zone/stretch play. Basic gap blocking includes an onside blocker blocking down, another blocker kicking out, and a third blocker leading through the point of attack. The popular "counter-trey" play is a classic example of a play used in this type of offense.

To defend against these plays in the basic defense, a team must simply make its reads and play its gap control in an aggressive fashion. Particularly important in defending against the gap blocking plays is the technique which involves having the defensive linemen come under all kick-out blocks. A critical factor when defending against zone blocking plays is the upfield charge of the defensive linemen versus the reach block.

A pro style offense utilizes a variety of formations. For the sake of simplicity, the following plays are illustrated in the standard pro formation with I backs (Diagrams 9-15 through 9-19).

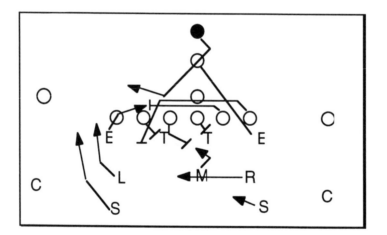

Diagram 9-15.
Counter trey.

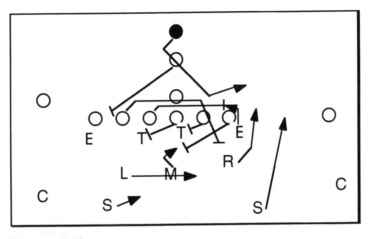

Diagram 9-16.
Weakside counter trey.

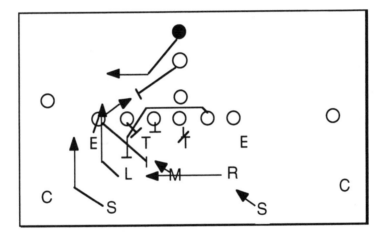

Diagram 9-17.
Power.

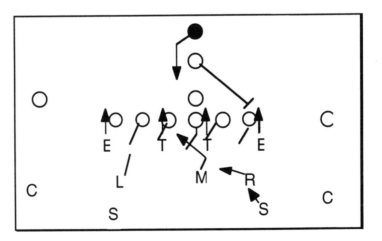

Diagram 9-18.
Inside zone.

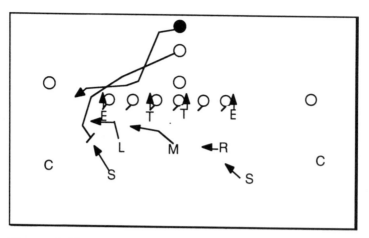

Diagram 9-19.
Outside zone/stretch.

The 4-3 defense handles most option plays from the pro style offense quite easily. This defense has a safety on both flanks to play the pitch. It also has an outside linebacker who lines up outside of the offensive tackle on each side of the offensive formation. This alignment enables the defense, in most cases, to get four defenders in the perimeter when defending the option play (Diagrams 9-20 and 9-21).

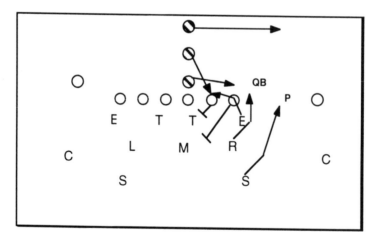

Diagram 9-20.
Weakside inside veer.

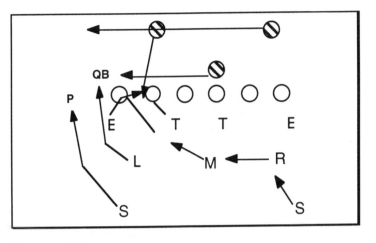

Diagram 9-21.
Y side outside veer.

The most difficult option play to defend occurs when the offense utilizes the threat of the dump pass to the tight end on an inside veer play to the tight-end side. The outside release by the tight end naturally changes the assignments (Diagram 9-22).

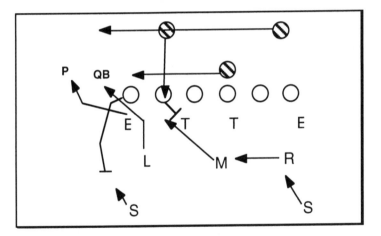

Diagram 9-22.

If this change is difficult, a specific adjustment can be made (Diagram 9-23).

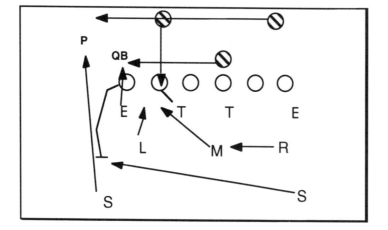

Diagram 9-23.

This adjustment is called "rotating the safeties to the option." The onside safety "hangs" briefly on the tight-end dump-pass route, then attacks the pitch responsibility. The backside safety runs immediately to the dump. With this tactic, the defense slows down the backside outside linebacker. This linebacker must now play the cutback or the reverse. If the offensive team has the dump pass threat, it is preferable to rotate the safeties. Diagram 9-24 illustrates another version of the inside veer with the dump pass threat and how to defend it by rotating the safeties.

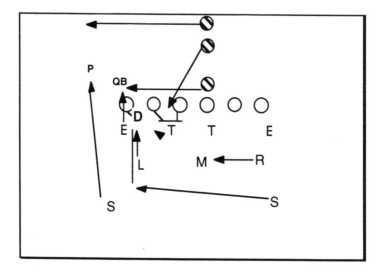

Diagram 9-24.
Rotating safeties vs. T dump threat.

The popular split-back "load sweep" can be outnumbered with proper execution of the defense to either side (Diagrams 9-25 and 9-26).

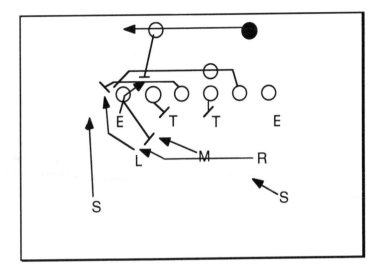

Diagram 9-25.
Y side load sweep.

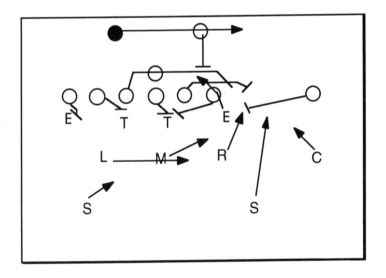

Diagram 9-26.
Weakside load sweep.

Trap and isolation plays were discussed earlier. The key to trap defense is the basic defensive lineman technique of coming under kick-out or trap blocks. The keys to defending against an isolation play are the reads and the reactions of the linebackers.

In defending against the passing game of the pro style offense, it is important to have several coverage variations and several types of blitzes. That type of variety is possible in the 4-3 defensive system. When applying this system to a particular pass offense, it is important to define the type of pass offense.

The pro style passing game can be divided into two types: schematic and match-up. The schematic style involves a series of pass plays designed to attack different coverages. In this approach, the quarterback will have a choice of receivers to throw to based upon how the pass defenders react after the ball is snapped. The coaches of these offenses often talk about stretching the defense either horizontally or vertically. For example, versus a standard zone coverage defense, the following pass pattern stretches the underneath coverage in a typical fashion (Diagram 9-27).

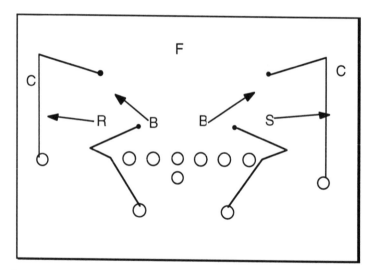

Diagram 9-27.

On either side of the formation, the quarterback can throw underneath the inside linebacker or over the top of the inside linebacker based upon the depth and location of his linebacker drop. A similar choice can be made on the outside of the formation (Diagram 9-28).

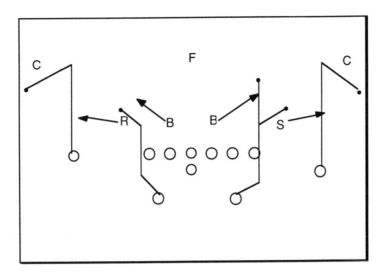

Diagram 9-28.

In this situation, the quarterback can throw to the wide receiver on an out-pass route or the inside receiver on a turn-out pass route. Using these principles and other similar ones, many pass plays can be designed.

The basic Cover 4 is very effective against these kinds of routes. The underneath coverage is unique. The linebackers are in a match-up zone coverage. They do not worry about inside or outside pass routes by the wide receivers, because the cornerbacks are responsible for those routes. The three linebackers cover pass routes by the three inside receivers. Pass patterns designed to stretch the underneath coverage are not effective because the linebackers are not responsible for defending the receivers on the outside (Diagrams 9-29 and 9-30).

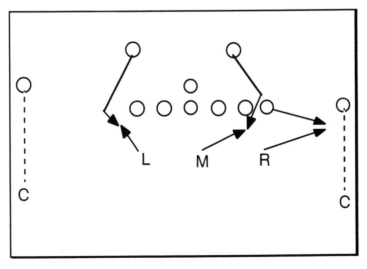

Diagram 9-29.

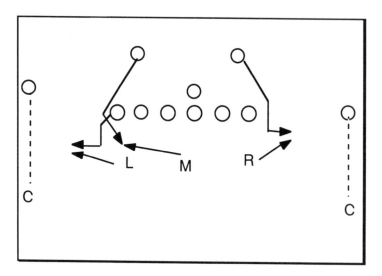

Diagram 9-30.

This unique feature in the underneath coverage is also very helpful in defending screen passes, delay passes, and draws. In this package, the linebackers are not worried about getting to any particular zone area. They are watching the three eligible inside receivers and playing their routes. Another important feature of the coverage is that it employs two safeties who will help any cornerback or linebacker who needs help in covering a deep pass route run by their receiver (Diagram 9-31).

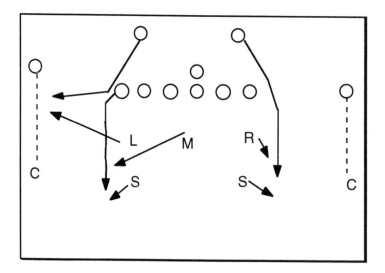

Diagram 9-31.

The basic Cover 4 is very good against schematic passing games. The match-up type of pass offense is cause for more concern. The defense could be overmatched with a better skilled wide receiver covered by a cornerback or a better skilled inside receiver covered by a linebacker. These match-ups vary from week to week and season to season.

A cornerback who is overmatched usually overplays the deep pass routes and consequently become very vulnerable to short and intermediate pass routes. A linebacker who is overmatched would face a similar dilemma.

The 4-3 defensive system has two solutions to this problem. A discussion regarding how to help a linebacker who "walks out" and covers a receiver in the slot alignment has previously been covered in this text. The safety deepens, thinks pass first, and focuses on helping the linebacker.

The preferred method of helping the overmatched cornerback is to put him up in a press alignment with bump-and-run techniques. The safety plays a loose technique which makes him more like a "halves" safety with less concern for the run. The cornerback can now jam the wide receiver, trail him on his pass patterns, and play tough on the underneath pass routes. He is more concerned with defending short pass routes because the safety is in position to help with deep-pass routes. This variation is preferable on passing downs.

The other solution is to blitz. A team can blitz on any down. In applying blitzes each week, it is important to analyze the pass protection scheme of the opponent. Very few high school teams use multiple protection schemes. Generally, we try to call the blitz that will put our defensive ends on the running backs. If the backs are responsible inside, we use the "fire" blitz. If the backs are responsible outside, we use the "dog" blitz. For a special blitz, we might bring a safety from the side opposite the center's block (Diagrams 9-32 and 9-33).

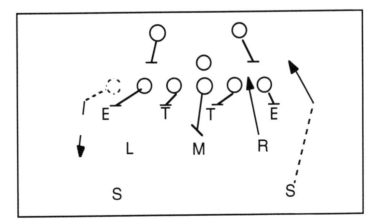

Diagram 9-32.
Safety blitz away from the center's block.

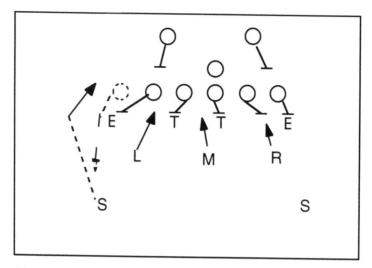

Diagram 9-33.

When blitzing, it is important for the pass rushers to recognize the quick-drop by the quarterback and to immediately get their hands and arms up in the throwing lanes. A standard tactic in defeating the blitz is the quick-drop passing game, which utilizes the quick-slant and the out-pass routes.

Whichever blitz is called, an outside rusher is always employed. Upon recognition of the quick-drop by the quarterback, the outside rusher is responsible for getting his hands in the air in the quick-out throwing lane. The adjacent inside rusher is responsible for getting his hands in the quick-slant throwing lane (Diagram 9-34).

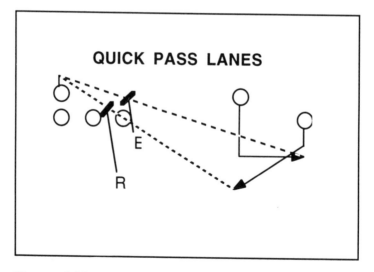

Diagram 9-34.

Regardless of the style of offensive attack, the defense can always switch to a two-deep or a three-deep zone coverage as a change of pace or to combat something with which the team is having trouble. Deep zone coverages, however, are rarely needed.

VERSUS THE RUN AND SHOOT

We use two methods to defend against spread formations. One is the "slash" mode in which we keep "seven in the box," play man coverage, and blitz to pressure any pass. The other is the "walk" mode in which we walk linebackers out, commit fewer defenders to rush the passer, and play run (but use more defenders in coverage).

The run-and-shoot offense is, perhaps, the most effective type of the various spread offenses. It utilizes one running back, no tight end, and four wide receivers. In keeping with our philosophy of defense, we have both a "slash" and "walk" mode ready for any run-and-shoot team we play.

At the beginning of this chapter, it was mentioned that a run-and-shoot team that also has a triple option play disfigures our base defense to some degree. This disfigurement comes when we are in our "walk" mode. In this mode, we play a three-deep zone coverage. We use our strong safety as a flat-zone player on one side and an outside linebacker as a flat-zone player on the other side. The two remaining linebackers balance up in the B gaps. Although it involves defending the run with only six players "in the box," any match-up problems versus the passing plays are avoided. It is safer, but softer, than our other mode.

This coverage is called Cover 3 Roll because the inside linebacker coverage is slid toward the trips. The free safety also moves over to the side of the trips to facilitate his run support responsibility (Diagram 9-35).

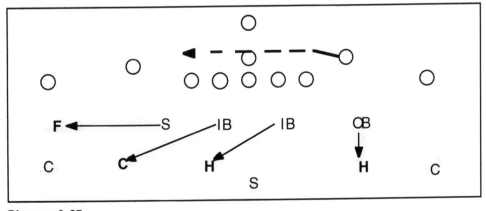

Diagram 9-35.
Roll to trips.

Since both linebackers are in the B gaps, both defensive tackles are put in the A gaps. In this situation, the defensive linemen do not have a directional call. This variation of the defense is called Flex Cover 3 Roll (Diagram 9-36). The word "flex" has no meaning relating to the defense. It is simply used to help identify this variation.

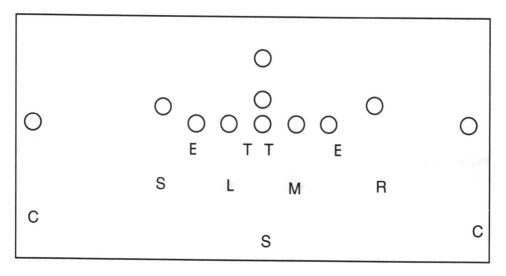

Diagram 9-36.
Flex cover 3 roll.

The players in the inside linebacker positions must read the guard and the tackle, just as Razor and Lazor do on a split-end side. This situation may require substituting for the Mike linebacker in this defense.

The two major running plays that must be stopped are the draw and the option. If the offense runs a triple option, these plays are more difficult to stop. A defensive scheme that is based upon the basic reads, however, can handle the triple option.

In our system, the run-and-shoot Ace back screen is classified as a running play because it must be stopped by the inside defenders. Both the screen and the draw are difficult plays for the 4-3 defense because the inside linebackers have pass-drop responsibilities. Consequently, the defense has to sacrifice pass rush pressure and "spy" both A gap tackles for screen and draw plays. Only after the threat of screen and draw have passed can the tackles rush the quarterback aggressively. The inside linebackers are looking back at the Ace back as they drop to their zones. They must be very aware of the Ace-back draw and screen. Upon recognition of these plays, the inside linebackers must plant their feet and charge the play. Another defender who should be in position to help on the Ace-back screen and draw is the flat defender away from the direction of the quarterback sprint. He also keys the Ace back as he takes his drop.

In defending the triple option, the natural reads versus a veer blocking scheme will put the defensive ends on the dive, the linebackers on the quarterback, and the flat defenders on the pitch. The reads versus a non-veer blocking scheme will put the linebackers on the dive and the defensive ends on the quarterback (Diagram 9-37).

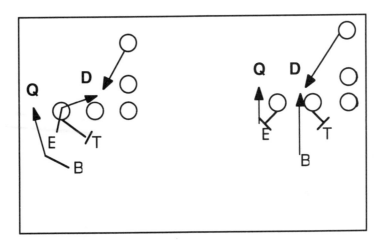

Diagram 9-37.
Natural reads.

The slot back will block either the inside linebacker or the flat defender, or he will release up to the free safety. If the slot back releases to the free safety, all the assignments remain intact. If he blocks a different player, the free safety now has the pitch. If he blocks inside on the inside linebacker, the flat defender takes the quarterback. Once these assignments have been mastered, the 4-3 defense can successfully take on the run-and-shoot running game (Diagrams 9-38 through 9-40).

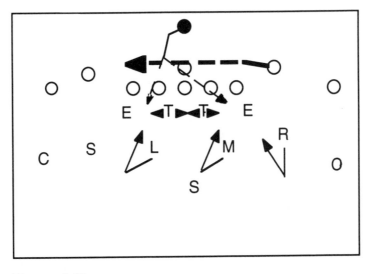

Diagram 9-38.
Ace draw.

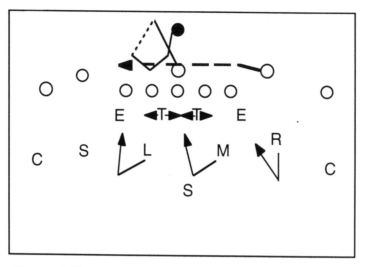

Diagram 9-39.
Ace screen.

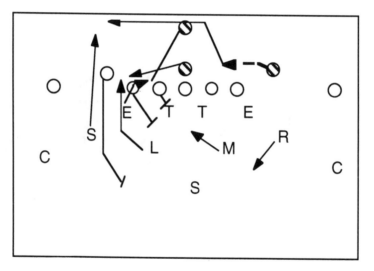

Diagram 9-40.
Ace triple option.

While defending the pass in the Flex Cover 3 defense, it is important to prevent the deep completion and avoid any "naked" man-to-man match-ups since there is minimal pressure on the quarterback. The run-and-shoot pass offense has a large number of plays. Diagram 8-41 illustrates how to cover one typical run-and-shoot pass play with the Cover 3 Roll coverage. The same coverage principles would apply to all run-and-shoot pass patterns.

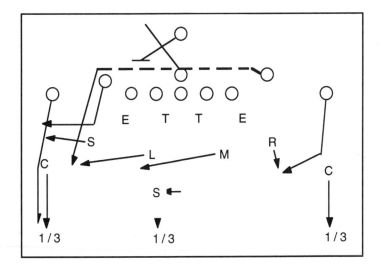

Diagram 9-41.
Basic run-and-shoot pattern vs. cover 3 roll.

In the "slash" mode, seven defenders remain "in the box." Consequently, the defense can put more pressure on the passing quarterback and play against both the draw and the screen much more easily. The perimeter defense versus the option is very similar to the flex defense. In both, the defense is able to get four defenders outside to the perimeter. Against the passing game, the "slash" mode is superior to the flex defense in defending the short and intermediate pass routes which are designed to find seams and holes in the zone defense. The weakness in the "slash" mode is the "naked" man-to-man coverage across the board. However, because of the hard six-man rush, the quarterback will normally not have much time to throw the ball. The defensive line can also execute line stunts to put further pressure on the passer. Only when the Mike linebacker is having trouble with the Ace-back draw is the defensive tackle away from the quarterback sprint asked to "spy" the draw.

Since it is not necessary to alter the basic concept with the inside front, it is important to have a directional call for the defensive linemen. If the ball is in the middle of the field, the direction is to the side of the quarterback's throwing arm. If the ball is on the hash mark, the direction is to the wide side of the field.

The Mike linebacker has the Ace back man-to-man, which is consistent with the basic defensive assignments versus any offense. The two outside linebackers are blitzing. If the quarterback sprints to a blitzer, that blitzer becomes the contain rusher. If the quarterback sprints away from a blitzer, the blitzer should flatten his rush so he can help on the draw and screen. Backside contain would be the responsibility of the defensive ends. An important aspect of the outside linebacker assignments is to cancel the quarterback on any option play. The path of the blitz charge is based upon the action of the quarterback (Diagram 9-42).

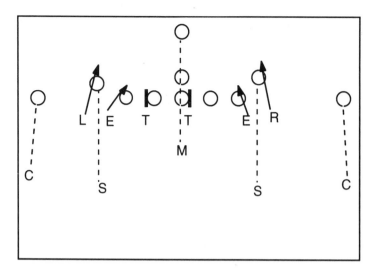

Diagram 9-42.
Basic "slash" vs. the run-and-shoot.

When the offense motions to a trips formation, the safeties rotate over and stay locked on their receivers. No one else changes. The safeties, however, must know that one of them must take the pitch on the option play. The only exception to that rule is if a wide receiver crack blocks on a safety. In that case, the cornerback covering the wide receiver would take the blocked safety's pitch assignment.

In this situation, the safeties have additional coverage assignments. If the slot-back being covered blocks the blitzing outside linebacker, the safety comes up to play the quarterback. Aside from the safeties, the defensive players have very simple assignments. For the defense to be effective, the seven inside defenders must be very aggressive, and the cornerbacks need to cover the wide receivers with great intensity (Diagrams 9-43 through 9-46).

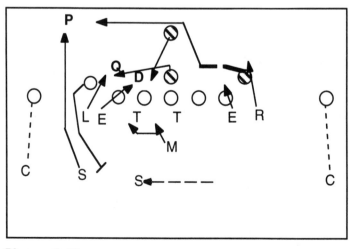

Diagram 9-43.
Vs. wing arc inside SS.

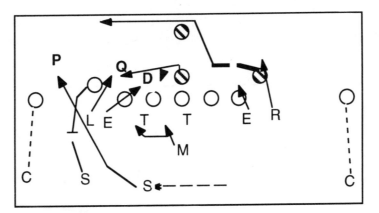

Diagram 9-44.
Vs. wing arc outside SS.

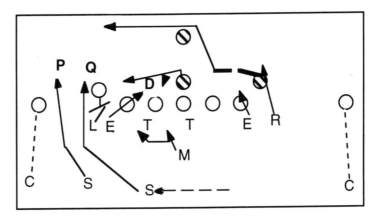

Diagram 9-45.
Vs. wing load OLB.

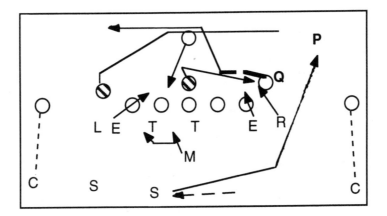

Diagram 9-46.
Vs. motion counter option.

Defending the inside running game is not difficult, primarily because the Mike linebacker does not drop to a zone, but mirrors the Ace back (Diagrams 9-47 through 9-49).

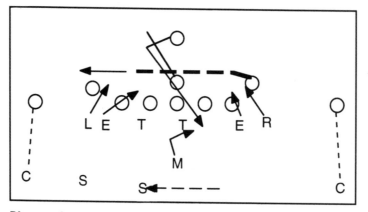

Diagram 9-47.
Ace draw.

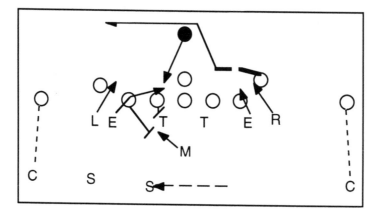

Diagram 9-48.
Ace dive.

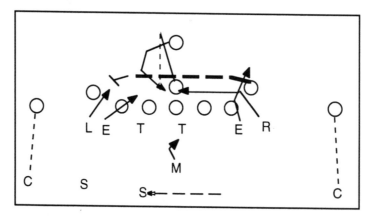

Diagram 9-49.
Ace screen.

As discussed earlier, pass defense in this coverage is simple and aggressive, but somewhat vulnerable to match-up problems (Diagram 9-50).

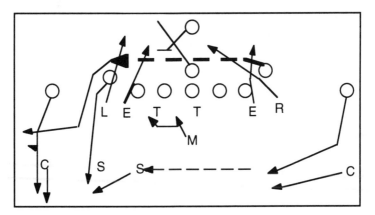

Diagram 9-50.
"Slash" vs. typical run-and-shoot pattern.

We feel comfortable playing the run-and-shoot offense if we have the "slash" and "walk" modes ready for action. On the other hand, we adhere to this philosophy of defense every week against any offense.

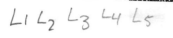

-3 Package

| on the 4-3 defense—goal line defense,
ule. Each of these areas are essential if
ented into your program.

he 4-3 defense is its simplicity in alignments. It is not a multiple defense, the defensive linemen do not have to spend very much time learning where to line up. As a result, these linemen can devote a great deal of time working on their fundamental skills and techniques. Taking the time to teach an entirely different front for goal line situations would be both contradictory to the philosophy of the 4-3 defense and a counterproductive way of spending the time and energies of our team.

Once we adopted the 4-3 as our fundamental defense, we discard the 6-5 goal line defense that we used previously. In a goal line situation, the strategies and techniques that are integral to our 4-3 defensive packages (and combinations thereof) are applied to whatever offensive scheme we are defending.

It is important to understand the combination of strategies and variations that already exists in our 4-3 defensive system. We refer to one such variation as our "Bear" defense (Diagram 10-1). It involves a defensive front change-up that has been derived from reducing down on the open-end side and bringing up a linebacker to the L.O.S. and rushing him. Additional teaching points on the "Bear" defense concerning linebacker alignments, secondary coverages, and the tight end-side defensive end techniques were presented in Chapter 8.

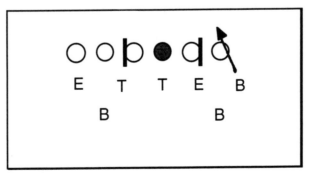

Diagram 10-1.
The "Bear" defense.

The "Bear" defense is the only defensive front variation that we employ. Although it's simple, it's a very effective change-up, particularly against opponents who want to attack inside at the three linebacker bubbles of our defense. The "Bear" defense also serves as an excellent short-yardage defense and as one that can be used in goal line situations.

An option we like even better in goal line situations involves combining the "Bear" defensive front with our "Basic" defense. To do this, a defensive back is taken out and replaced with an extra defensive lineman (Diagram 10-2). We call this defense "Buzzard." It is actually a great deal like our basic defense, but with an extra tackle.

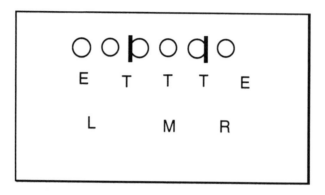

Diagram 10-2.
The "Buzzard" defense.

The reads and the alignments for both the linebackers and the defensive ends in the "Buzzard" defensive scheme are identical to what we employ in our "Basic" defense. Both defensive tackles play the 3 technique they normally use on the tight-end side. The nose tackle plays head-up on the offensive center, keeping his arm free to the open-end side.

Although the "Buzzard" defense presents a very good front, it has a drawback in the secondary. We cannot play our Cover 4 with only three defensive backs. Many of the teams we face, however, use a double-tight end formation, our Cover 4 can be emulates with only three defensive backs. One cornerback is taken out, and both safeties are left in the game (Diagram 10-3).

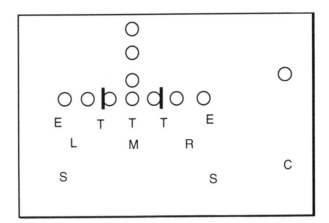

Diagram 10-3.
Secondary alignments in the "Buzzard" defense.

In our "Buzzard" defense, the defensive backs play exactly as they do in Cover 4, including having the safeties provide run support. As a result, against the very popular double-tight end goal line formation, the "Buzzard" offer an excellent goal line defense, with very little new teaching.

In a goal line situation, an important factor is to closely study your opponent's formation and substitution system. If your opponent is still in a two-wide receiver formation, the "Buzzard" is not as effective. If you use "Buzzard" in that situation, both cornerbacks should be kept in the game. Because the single safety who is left in the game must be the "force" player on both sides, you lose your cut-back defender (Diagram 10-4).

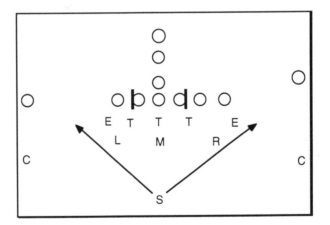

Diagram 10-4.
The "Buzzard" defense against a two-wide receiver formation.

Although we have sometimes used this form of "Buzzard" deployment on the goal line against a two-wide receiver formation, we prefer to employ other tactics, including "basic dog," "basic fire," and "bear defense." On occasion, we also use secondary blitzes when we're backed-up deep against our goal line. Diagrams 10-5 and 10-6 illustrate our blitzes involving cornerbacks and safeties, respectively.

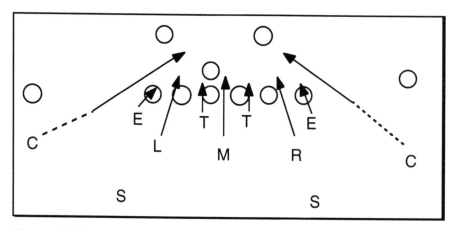

Diagram 10-5.
The cornerback.

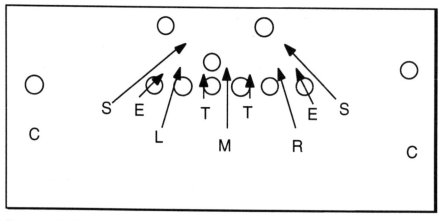

Diagram 10-6.
The safety blitz is called a "Stinger Dog."

Drills for the 4-3 Defense

In addition to the basics types of football drills that are used by most all football teams to develop defensive fundamentals, we employ several drills that are specifically designed to enhance our ability to play our basic Cover 4 defense.

The first drill we use is designed for the Cover 4 safeties. Called the "Flank" drill, this drill involves a scout backfield, a scout tight end, and two scout wide receivers. The drill is set with two safeties facing a pro formation (Diagram 10-7).

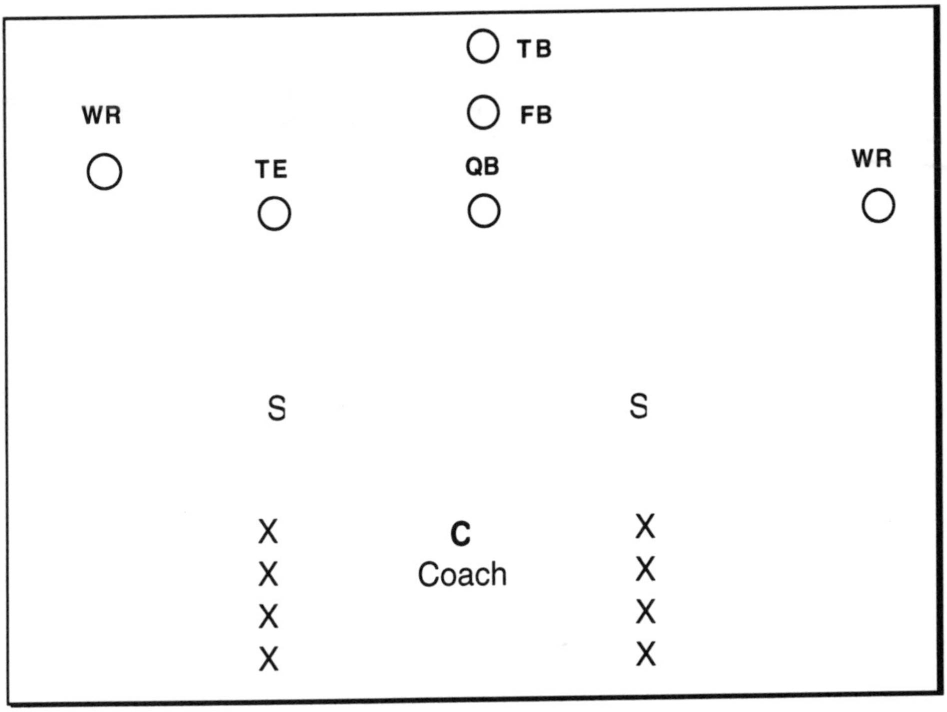

Diagram 10-7.
Two safeties aligned in the "Flank" drill.

We run four plays to each side of the formation: the sweep, the cutback, the wide receiver reverse, and a play-action pass with the tight end blocking. The two safeties are given numerous repetitions on these plays until they develop the ability to react quickly and naturally to each play (Diagram 10-8 through 10-11). Each play must be run to both sides of the formation.

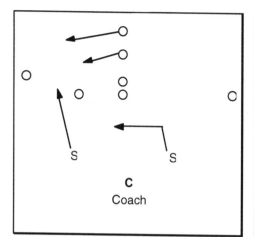

Diagram 10-8.
Reacting to the sweep play.

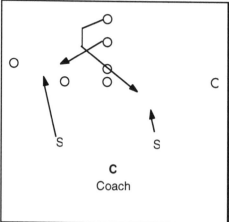

Diagram 10-9.
Reacting to the cutback play.

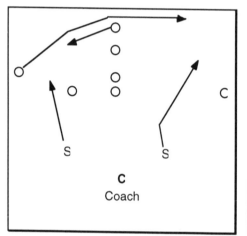

Diagram 10-10.
Reacting to the reverse play.

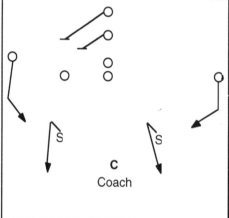

Diagram 10-11.
Reacting to a play-action pass.

The second drill in our package of drills for the 4-3 defense is designed for linebackers. While all teams have "read" drills for their linebackers, our linebackers employ reads that are a little more complex. For example, in our 4-3 defense, the Razor and Lazor linebackers read the two adjacent offensive linemen before they look for the ball. The Mike linebacker reads the fullback to the guard. Teams have used these types of reads for years. Although they're not revolutionary, these reads are not simple. As a result, we test our linebackers on their reads *every single day*. To accomplish this, we use separate read drills. One is for the Mike linebacker, while the other is for the Razor linebacker (Diagram 10-12 and 10-13).

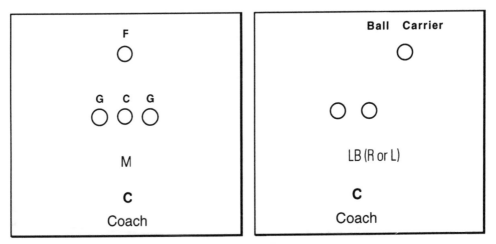

Diagram 10-12.
Inside linebacker read drill.

Diagram 10-13.
Outside linebackers read drill.

By utilizing two coaches and holding two separate drills simultaneously, ten minutes each day, the linebackers get the practice repetitions they need to get the job done. As a matter of philosophy, we rarely make changes, if any, in the linebacker reads from week to week.

The defensive linemen also need to master their read-on-the-run reactions with daily drills. One of these drills is a little unique, yet very crucial to the development of the essential fundamentals. Called the "Rake-Through" drill, this drill is set up with five large bags (i.e., blocking dummies) positioned five yards apart in a straight line. The bags are held in place by players unless the bags are pop-up bags (Diagram 10-14).

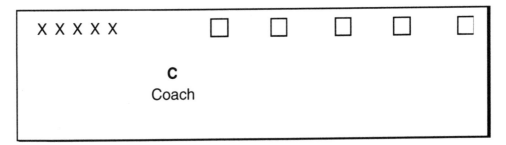

Daigram 10-14.
The starting set up for the "Rake-Through" drill.

The drill begins by having the linemen "get off" on a signal by the coach. They perform the drill by proceeding down the line of bags. At the first four bags, they execute a series of low-to-high arm rips, while alternating arms. Each arm rip is finished with the lineman's fist above his head. As the defensive linemen approach the last (fifth) bag, they dip down and run through the bag while tackling it (Diagram 10-15).

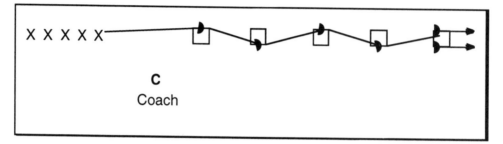

Diagram 10-15.
The action sequence for the rake-through drill.

The "Rake-Through" drill teaches defensive linemen to "rip and run," so they can learn to defeat blocks and keep running. The blocks could be hook blocks, kick-out blocks, or pass blocks. Regardless, the drill involves having the defenders attack the blocks and run through them to the ball carrier because in our defensive scheme, it is essential that we have defensive linemen who are aggressive and active to make plays.

The final drill to be covered in this chapter is a team drill that we call the "Blue Devil" drill. More than anything else, this drill is designed to teach an aggressive attitude about team defense. All of our defensive coaches coach this drill—and coach it hard. The attitude that is emphasized in the drill is one of determination to disengage from blockers so that the defenders can run at full speed to hit the ball carrier.

The drill involves having the players line up, single file, in front of each of the five bags which have been placed on the five-man blocking sled. The brakes on the portable blocking sled are set on by coach #1 in order to keep the sled from moving. Five, large upright bags are positioned, in a single row, to the right and diagonally to the row of bags on the sled. Each bag in the diagonal line corresponds to a bag on the sled. All of the bags used in the drill (those on the sled and those on the ground) are blue—hence the name of the drill. The first player in each of the five lines then assumes his football stance approximately one yard from the sled (Diagram 10-16).

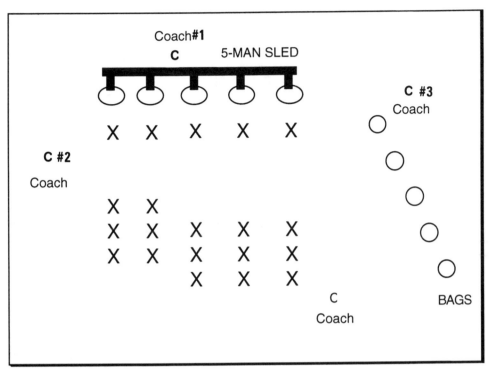

Diagram 10-16.
The starting set up for the "Blue-Devil" drill.

Coach #2 starts the drill with a visual movement of a football. Upon movement of the football, all five players step up and strike the sled with a two-hand shiver. They immediately lock out their arms and run in place as hard and as fast as they can until they hear the next whistle. After four to five seconds, the coach blows his whistle which signals all five players to leave the sled and attack their corresponding large upright bag. They run full speed to their bag, hit it with a low-to-high technique, rap their arms around the bag, and continue sprinting another five steps while lifting the bag into the air. Each player then resets his bag to the upright position and the drill continues with the next player in each line (Diagram 10-17).

Half way through the drill, the upright bags are positioned to the left of the bags on the blocking sled, and the drill continues—only in the left direction. All coaches are positioned in and around the drill to vigorously urge the players to go full speed for every "milli-second" the players are participating in the drill. The atmosphere around this drill is vigorous, spirited, and intense. With continued repetitions, this drill can also become an excellent conditioner. We use the drill on a daily basis usually for short periods of time. On occasion, however, we extend the length of time that the drill is run, depending upon our conditioning schedule.

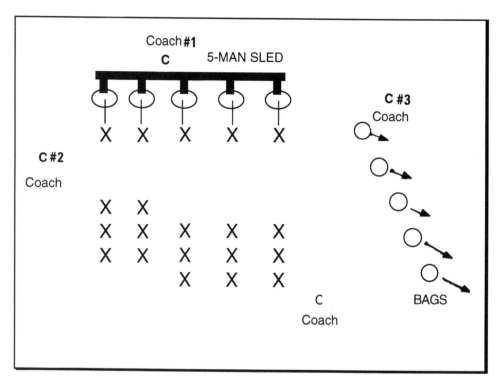

Diagram 10-17.
The action sequence for the "Blue-Devil" drill.

Practice Schedule

Our approach to organizing and scheduling practices has three salient features. First, we are a two-platoon football team. We have a complete set of defensive players and coaches and a complete set of offensive players and coaches. We have embraced this philosophy for many years and have been very successful with it. With our two-platoon system, more players get playing time during games. As a result, we get more players trying out for the varsity football team. We usually have a relatively good number of players on our football quad. We realize that the best eleven players on the team may not always be in the game at the same time. However, the players who are on the field will be thoroughly prepared, drilled, and conditioned. One of the most important benefits of our two-platoon system is that it enables us to have a lot of time to coach our players. As a consequence, if we organize our practice schedules carefully, we should have players who are fundamentally sound and a system that is capable of having some complexities to it.

Second, our practice schedules feature a repetitious daily routine. Our practice periods and times are the same each day and vary little from day-to-day or week-to-week. We want our players and coaches to always know what drill period they are in, where they are supposed to be, and what skills they are developing. The only change in our schedule will be determined by the amount of protective gear that our players are required to wear to practice.

Finally, we strongly believe in "relevance." *All drills must have relevance!* We do not go out and run around some cones just for the sake of running around cones. We discuss and analyze every drill that we use. Our drills must relate to specific aspects of football that we use and teach in our football system. This philosophy has caused us to re-evaluate our complete football drills, but relative only to a traditional 3-4 defense and not our 4-3 defense are no longer practiced. Tables 10-1 and 10-2 provide examples of sample practice schedules without and with pads respectively.

Table 10-1. Sample practice schedule conducted in shorts and helmet.

	LB	Sec.	DL
PRE-PRACTICE PERIOD (30 Minutes)	Reads Man cover Zone cover	Footwork Fund. Cushion Ball Drills	Get-off & Pursue Rake Through Reads-Arm Bags
TEAM CALISTHENICS PERIOD (5 Minutes)	W h o l e T e a m		
GROUP PERIOD (25 Minutes)	10 Minutes- 15 Minutes- **LB** vs. Inside Run with DL	All Defense-"Blue Devil" Drill **Sec.** Coverage Review Flank Drill Press cover	 **DL** vs. Inside Run with LBs
7 ON 7 PERIOD (30 Minutes)	**LB** Pass Defense vs Opponents Offense	**Sec.**	**DL** Pass Rush 2 man sled Reads-Arm Bags
TEAM PERIOD (40 Minutes)	1) Formation Review with Bear & Basic 2) Blitz Review 3) "Perimeter" Run and "Play Action" Pass vs. Bear & Basic		
TEAM CONDITIONING (10 Minutes)	W h o l e T e a m 8 x 100 Striders		

Table 10-2. Sample practice schedule conducted in full gear.

	LB	Sec.	DL
PRE-PRACTICE PERIOD (30 Minutes)	Reads Man cover Zone cover Tackling	Footwork Fund. Cushion Ball Drills Tackling	Get-off & Pursue Rake Through Tackling
TEAM CALISTHENICS PERIOD (5 Minutes)	W h o l e T e a m		
GROUP PERIOD (25 Minutes)	10 Minutes- 15 Minutes- **LB** Bear Reads vs. Inside Run with DL	All Defense-"Blue Devil" Drill **Sec.** Flank Drill Press cover Coverage Review	 **DL** Reads vs. Inside Run with LBs
7 ON 7 PERIOD (30 Minutes)	**LB** **Sec.** Pass Defense vs Opponents Offense		**DL** Pass Rush 2 man sled 1 vs. 1 with OL

TEAM PERIOD (40 Minutes)	1) Blitz Review
	2) Scout Team with "perimeter" Run
	    and "play action" Pass emphasis
	3) LIVE SCRIMMAGE
	    Short Yardage & Goal line vs. Offense		

TEAM CONDITIONING (10 Minutes)	W h o l e T e a m Speed Drills		

Tim Simons has served as head football coach for the Clovis High School Cougars in Clovis, California for twenty-one years. The success of the Clovis High School football program is reflected by Coach Simons' record of 193-50-4. During his tenure he has led Clovis High School to seven section finals, three section championships, and ten conference championships. He was selected the 1984 California State High School Football Coach of the Year, and the 1991 Northern California High School Coach of the Year.

He has earned numerous central California awards and honors and is a popular clinic speaker. He has spoken at football clinics in San Francisco, Los Angeles, San Diego, Fresno, Seattle, Reno, St. Louis and Atlantic City.

Mike Freeman has served as an assistant coach at Clovis High School for twenty years. Prior to his arrival at CHS he spent three years at San Joaquin Memorial High School (Fresno, California) where he served as defensive coordinator coach. He excelled as a defensive player in college while playing cornerback for Fresno State University. He was selected as a member of the 1968 college All-star team that played the world champion Green Bay Packers. Coach Freeman's professional playing career included three years with the Atlanta Falcons in the National Football League. In 1972, he returned to central California to begin his high school coaching career which includes coaching contributions to three section championships at Clovis High School and one section championship at San Joaquin Memorial High School.

ADDITIONAL FOOTBALL RESOURCES FROM